How to Sell Coaching

(and Get More Coaching Clients)

CGW
PUBLISHING

2020

How to Sell Coaching

(and Get More Clients)

First Edition: August 2020

ISBN 978-1-908293-56-5

Published by:

CGW Publishing
B 1502
PO Box 15113
Birmingham
B2 2NJ
United Kingdom

www.cgwpublishing.com

mail@cgwpublishing.com

Genius

genius.coach

peter@genius.coach

genius.li/linkedin

genius.li/twitter

genius.li/facebook

Contents

Exercises

1:   Let's Cut to the Chase

To get more coaching clients, you need know only three things:

1. Your coaching will not sell itself, no matter how amazing you think you are

2. A client will not find out how good a coach you are until they have first experienced how good a salesperson you are

3. Sales is an equal exchange of value

That's it. You can stop reading now. Go away and think about this. And if you can't figure out how those three points will help you to get more coaching clients then I have included the rest of this book, at absolutely no additional cost, for your convenience and enjoyment.

Read on, and all shall be revealed.

1. Your coaching will not **SELL** itself, no matter how **AMAZING** you think you are

2. A client will not find out how good a **COACH** you are until they have first experienced how good a **SALESPERSON** you are

3. Sales is an **EQUAL** exchange of value

2:   Welcome

Learning is an investment in the future.

It's an investment in you, and it's an investment in your business.

Without learning, you would have to figure everything out by trial and error, and when other people have figured things out for you, it's wise to benefit from their knowledge.

Knowledge defines our culture. The rise of technologies such as the printing press, the television, mobile phones, the internet and social media demonstrate how much we like and need to acquire and share knowledge. Our survival depends on knowledge.

Learning isn't an accident, though. It's an organised, predictable process.

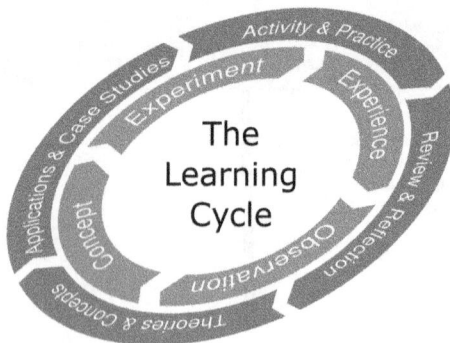

The Learning Cycle

People say, "practice makes perfect", however, this isn't strictly true. It's more accurate to say, "practice makes permanent". So practice isn't in itself important, what you must do is practice the right things.

In this book, which you can think of as a workshop in itself, I'm not going to say much about technology, for the simple reason that the people who say that technology enables sales are of course the people selling the technology. In my view, which you may or may not agree with, technology can be a barrier to sales, particularly when sales people rely on technology instead of having real conversations. Using client data to personalise your junk emails is not a relationship. Building an awesome sales funnel with mock webinars which are really just recorded videos is not building client engagement. Picking up the phone or, better, meeting people at events and interest groups – that's the start of a relationship.

Above all else, remember this: You are a salesperson.

If you have ever told someone that you run your own business, or you're a business owner, or even an entrepreneur, then you cannot hide from the fact that you are responsible for growing your business through sales. I'm sure you're an amazing coach, or consultant, or trainer, but you're not at that stage yet. If you want to get more clients, you have to think like a salesperson.

You have to become the salesperson, grasshopper.

3:   What is Sales?

Sales is... well, what do you think it is?

3.1.1   Sales

What does 'selling' mean?

What is the purpose of selling?

How does a client see a salesperson?

For our purposes, let's assume the following:

What does 'selling' mean?

Selling is an equal exchange of value in which clients agree to give you money in exchange for you providing them with a product or service.

What is the purpose of selling?

Its purpose is to manage that exchange in a controlled way so that you can predict and therefore influence the client's transaction.

How does a client see a salesperson?

As a barrier? As someone who will make me buy something I don't want? As a gatekeeper? 20 years ago, the salesperson was the client's source of knowledge. Now that place has been taken by Google and the salesperson's role is to guide the client through the complex ordering process. The salesperson might have knowledge which adds value to that process, but first has to earn the right to apply that knowledge.

Let's say that sales is an organised approach to guiding a potential client through a decision process which ends with that client paying money for, and receiving, a product or service.

There are two sides to sales:

- Strategy, which is what you do before you talk to a prospective client

- Tactics, which is what you do when you're talking to a prospective client

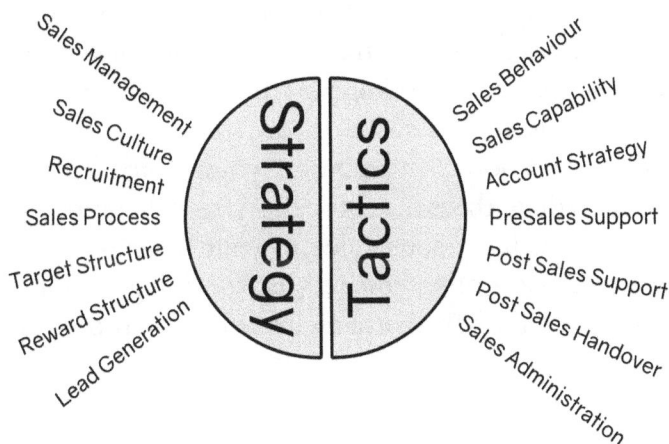

What you have to do is make sure you're doing the right things at the right times. Some sales people say that they're a creative, dynamic, responsive sales virtuoso who likes to be flexible. In other words, they have no plan and are working reactively, which means the client is calling the shots, which means they'll never be in control of the deal. The best sales people I've ever met are not super-slick smooth talkers, they are simply the most organised, pragmatic, analytical people I've ever met.

And by 'best', of course I mean sales results. After all, your job as a sales person is to secure new business. In some companies, sales targets are very complicated, with metrics for client satisfaction, client retention, product types, service delivery and so on. In any business, it's important to balance short term income with long term growth, so any good sales person will always deliver business that is good today and for the future.

Every activity in your day needs to ultimately lead to client income, whether that comes from delivering a coaching session, sending an invoice, building your website, posting on social media, running a webinar, writing a book, updating your profile… by understanding the sales process, you will understand how every activity adds value to your business. It isn't then a question of whether it's worth doing or not, it's a question of when that activity converts into cash in the bank.

You might think that it's not all about money, you might think that your coaching work is a gift or a calling and you shouldn't need to worry about such things as money. If that were true, you wouldn't be reading this. Also, if you're lucky enough to be in a position where you don't need to earn money, you still need to remember that money itself is just a way of measuring and exchanging value. Even if you don't charge money for your work, you still need your time and expertise to be valued.

If you just want to know the secret to being a great sales person then here it is: make sure you're doing the right things at the right times. I know I've already said that, but that really is all there is to it. The trick is to know what the right thing is, and to figure out when the right time is.

4: Excellent Salespeople

What are the qualities of a great salesperson?

They might include:

- Energetic

- Likeable

- Enthusiastic

- Confident

- Intelligent

- Tenacious

- Knowledgeable

- Good communicators

- Persuasive

- Influential

- Credible

- Friendly

- ?

In fact, probably the most important quality of a great salesperson is that they are **organised**.

Everything else on that list is nice, but ultimately irrelevant. We all buy from salespeople who we don't like, who are dull and disengaged, because we don't actually care about the salesperson, we only care about getting our hands on the thing we want.

4.1.1   Your greatest asset

As a salesperson, what is your single most valuable asset?

I've modelled the very best sales people in all kinds of industries, which means that I have analysed their perceptions, thought processes and behaviours to figure out how they do what they do. The result is always that the very best sales people see their most valuable asset as their own time. Their respect for their own time makes them focus on what they can win and it gives the appearance of them respecting the client's time too. So that's good all round.

Your business has a business plan, including a set of goals and some ideas for how you're going to achieve those goals. But in between those future goals and your present reality is a gap, and that gap is going to be filled by sales people. In business, it's not the big that eat the small, it's the fast that eat the slow. As Charles Darwin pointed out, the species that are most successful are the ones most able to adapt to change, and in global recessions, we have seen time after time that the companies that survive and grow aren't the biggest or best, they're the ones that could react and adapt most quickly, turning a threat into an opportunity to change and thrive.

For almost 30 years, I have been working with sales leaders and sales teams, and the most common problem that I find, the most common reason that sales teams don't perform as well as they could, is that the behaviour of sales people is not aligned with the business plan, and that is absolutely the job of the sales manager.

Most companies engage sales training to change sales peoples' behaviour, however I have found that behaviour is almost never the problem; it's one of measurement and focus.

People who don't work in sales often think that success in sales comes from being confident, gregarious, chatty and so on. Ethereal qualities which you are born with but can't learn. Actually, these qualities are usually counter-productive in sales. All style and no substance, and so on.

You can easily learn the principles of sales operations and sales management and apply them in your coaching practice to get more consistent, predictable results.

4.2 Behaviour and Results

Probably the majority of sales managers, particularly when results aren't as good as they should be, focus on managing behaviour. Whilst these sales managers would never like to admit it, their underlying belief is, "I would have closed that deal if it had been mine. If these people just do what I tell them to do, everything will work properly." It's an illusion of control; if I could control everything then the world would be a better place.

Examples of a focus on behaviour are:

1. Make 20 sales calls per day

2. Send out 30 brochures per week

3. Follow the sales script

4. Tell the client three benefits

5. Leave the client with a free sample

The downsides of the controlling manager's belief are that it puts a great deal of pressure on the sales manager to be perfect, and it means that sales people aren't responsible for their results. They follow orders, and it isn't their fault if those orders don't produce results.

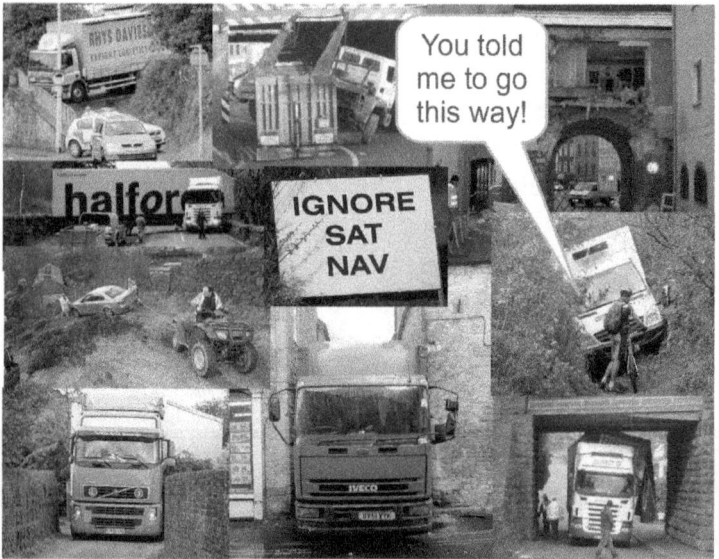

The alternative to this is a focus on results. When you hold people accountable for achieving results, you also have to give them some freedom in how they achieve those results.

Examples of a focus on results include:

- Deliver £5m in new client revenue

- Create 10 new partner relationships

- 50% of revenue from new clients

However, you need to decide what you want those results to cost you. Let's say that you hit your sales target, but with an enormous expenses bill. If your expenses don't come out of your salary, why should you care? At the extreme, you might think that you

---

don't care what happens to the rest of the business as long as you're on target.

The senior managers at a large defence engineering business thought this way, and they ended up throwing more and more contractors at the problem of poor project management, where the cost of under-performance was at least £16 Million per year, including contractor costs and penalty payments which meant that the company would have made more profit if it hadn't won any contracts.

The managers of a leading specialist retailer I've worked with focus on results, with the consequence that their store managers run their stores how they like and get paid far more than store managers in other retailers. Everyone is so busy chasing results that there is little consistency in how those results are delivered, and the business strategy changes from one month to the next as the MD gets impatient that the latest strategy isn't working quickly enough.

Focusing on results has a downside too. A results focus can encourage sales people to ignore the cost of achieving those results, and the cost of collateral damage can outweigh the benefits.

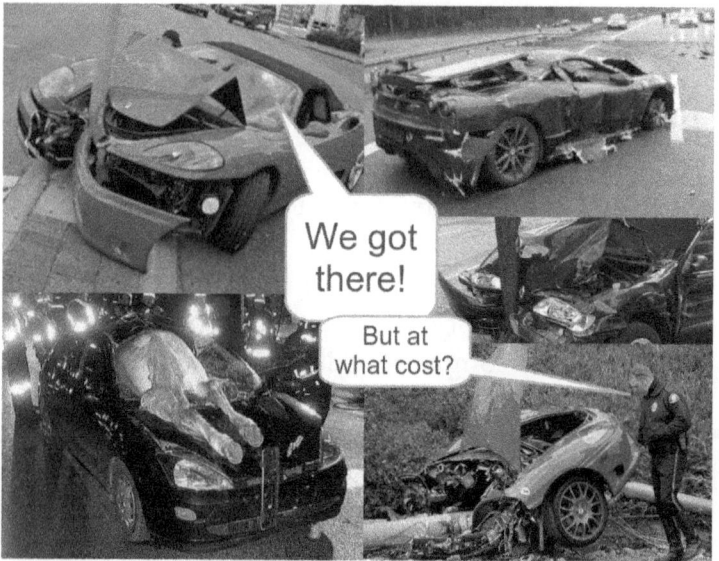

If you're a self employed, independent service provider such as a coach or trainer, why would you care what corporate sales people get up to?

If you haven't already worked out the links, allow me to point them out to you.

Behaviour focus

"I did everything right - but why don't I have enough clients?"

Results focus

"I won ten new clients - but why don't I have any money in the bank?"

4.3 The Best Sales People

The best sales people are very efficient time managers. They are focused and committed. And they do absolutely the minimum to get paid the maximum. Sales people really define a business, because they are the human face of it. They are the first people to speak to clients, and they create the first impression and set the client's expectations. It doesn't matter what your product or service is, your clients will learn about it from the way you behave in those early sales interactions.

If you are on time, honest, reliable and helpful, the client will automatically assume that this is way that everyone in your business will behave. They will expect your products to be reliable. They will expect your website to be honest. They will expect your client service to be helpful. The client learns everything about your company from their first interaction with you.

And if you not sure about a product, or you say something just to get the client to place an order, or if you forget to mention some anticipated problems with delivery, or if you don't send information when you promise to, your client will automatically assume that your products and services will be unreliable, that they can't trust what anyone says, that they can't count on you.

When a client buys from you, they are not buying because they think you are nice, or because your service looks interesting, or because they have nothing better to do. They are buying from you because they expect you to add value to their business. They expect you to solve a real problem that costs them real money. They expect you to help them respond to new opportunities. They expect you to do what you say you will do. They expect to be able to count on you.

I said that the best sales people are very efficient, and actually some people would say that they are lazy. But this is quite normal and it's a good thing, because it means that they really understand their business very well. They are hired to do a very simple job, and paid when they do that job well. So the very best sales people learn how to do that job as well as they can, and with the least effort possible. Sales people are very important in a business because, every day, they are testing the market and getting real feedback from clients. But that doesn't mean that they should decide on product or pricing strategy. Anyone can give a product away, but only an expert can create real value. Most importantly, you learn more from the people who don't buy from you than from the people who do.

The first and most important secret of the best salespeople is that they know that their single most valuable asset is their own time. All of these secrets actually arise from this first one.

Valuing their own time makes them qualify hard. In fact, they're almost ruthless. When they first speak to a potential client, they find out if they're talking to the decision maker, what the budget is, who the competitors are and so on. Yes, we all know that we should ask those questions, but it's often easier not to because it's uncomfortable to ask a question when you don't want to know the answer. But why would a sales person not want to know about the client's budget? Because if the client says that they don't have a budget, the sales person has to find someone else to talk to. If they don't ask, they can be busy without having to worry about being productive. They can send out brochures and go to meetings and never have to worry about their results. The best sales people understand how to measure their results.

The second secret is that they take personal responsibility for what they do and the results they get.

The very best sales people don't blame their competitors or products when they lose a sale – they know that there is only one reason to lose, because they didn't do enough to win it. This responsibility makes them connect their behaviour with their results. They don't rely on chance and luck, they rely on their own knowledge and skills.

The third secret is that they focus their time and effort on what they can control.

They don't fool themselves into thinking that they can control the client's decision, but they do know that they can ask questions, solve problems and anticipate objections so that they can control as many variables as possible. They try to take all of the uncertainty out of the sales cycle, or as much as they can. If they know they're not going to win a deal, or they can see that a competitor clearly has a better solution, they qualify out, walk away and spend their valuable time doing something that will bring them real results.

The fourth secret is that they prioritise based on hard, rational business criteria.

Average sales people prioritise based on what's easy or comfortable, or what they like doing, or what makes them feel good. They put off unpleasant tasks, where the best sales people treat every job the same. Why? Because they know that every job, from making cold calls to taking a client out to lunch is just one step in a much bigger journey. When the best sales people prioritise, they're always consistent. They don't sit at their desks, wondering what to do today. They already know.

The fifth secret is that they value the client relationship over the sale.

If they can't deliver the right solution for the client, they say so. They don't waste their own time, or their client's trying to make the wrong solution fit. They are honest, saying, "we can't help you this time, but I'd like to keep talking to you about projects that we're better suited to". They tell the client the truth, and that makes the client trust them more. They don't look for a 'quick win' that will only make the client unhappy, they would rather walk away this time and win better and bigger business next time.

The sixth and final secret is that they always sell what the client needs, not what they want.

Rather than take the easy option and just give the client what they ask for, they ask tough, deep questions. They challenge the client. They even tell the client that they're wrong. They build trust and credibility, and when the client asks for their advice, they give it, honestly and directly. They know that if the client's ego gets in the way, then the deal wasn't fair or right anyway. They challenge the client to think deeper about their needs and address real business problems, and that makes the client do a better job for their business. By challenging the client's needs, they help the client to become stronger.

4.4   Summary

1. Time is their most important asset

2. Take responsibility for their results

3. Focus on what they can control

4. A relationship is more important than a sale

5. Prioritise tasks based on logic not emotion

6. Work hard to uncover the real needs

4.5   The Six Secrets for Coaches

1. Time is your most important asset

It's easy to fall into the trap of thinking that because you're busy, you're productive. You can fill every day with free webinars, tinkering with your website, contributing to coaching forums and posting in social media groups to impress other coaches. Are these activities bringing you clients? You think they're all important, right? But are they *measurably* bringing you new clients? Unless you test and measure, you don't know the true effect of the wording on your website.

If you pay for advertising, you'll have a very clear incentive to test different adverts and focus your money on what generates the best results. Why not measure the effectiveness of your time in the same way?

2. Your results are your responsibility

If you fail to 'win' a client, it's not because they couldn't afford it, or your coaching was too expensive, or because you didn't have enough certificates, or because of the recession, or because of bad luck. It's because you didn't focus on the outcome and qualify the client's buying position. You didn't ask the hard questions. You were happy just because the client was talking to you and consuming your free advice.

3. Focus on what you can control

You cannot control the client's decision, you cannot control the market, you cannot control what your competitors are doing. You can only control your actions and the questions that you ask. If you are concerned about your prospect's ability to pay your fees, ask them. They might not tell you, and they might not tell you the truth, but you can only ask. By asking, you're at least communicating your expectations and needs, and you have more chance of making any transaction a fair and equal one.

4. A relationship is more important than a sale

If you're coaching and you're active on social media then you will no doubt be inundated with offers from marketing gurus who promise to get you dozens of new clients every week. Creating new leads is easy if you make empty promises or require contact details and email addresses in return for free resources. An email address is not a lead, and a client who is not the right fit for you is not a client at all.

When you can't help someone, or you don't want to help someone, point them in a more appropriate direction. You will benefit more from treating them well than from seeing them only as a source of money and delivering a service that is not up to your high standards. I've had referrals from people who I chose not to work with because they appreciated my ethics and my advice.

5. Prioritise tasks based on logic not emotion

There are many operational tasks that you enjoy doing, and there are many that you don't. One of my early mentors used to say to me, "John, you've got to take the rough with the smooth". I know what you're thinking - my name's not John.

6. Work hard to uncover the real needs

The easiest thing for you to say to a client is "yes" because you want their business. Your client will present their need or outcome to you, such as career coaching, or life change, or relationship improvements, and you'll say, "Yes! I can help you with that!" This sets an unrealistic expectation for a very simple reason. This isn't what the client actually wants. It's only what they're prepared to tell you before they have decided to trust you. If you don't uncover their real need in the first conversation with them, you will be focusing on the wrong outcome, and they will have a deeply unsatisfying experience of working with you.

4.6   Goals

We all have goals; some goals are explicit, we know what they are and we consciously work towards them, such as, "I want to get home on time today". Other goals are implicit, they guide our behaviour but we don't necessarily think about them, such as, "I want to feel like I've achieved something".

Your implicit goals shape your behaviour. They define how you answer the telephone, how you talk to a client, what questions you ask, and what you do when the client says, "I'll think about it."

Having clear outcomes, expressed in a certain way, actually makes it easier for you to achieve them. The following process is a way of refining your goals so that you can focus your time and energy on achieving them. As a coach, you are of course a master at goal setting. It's your bread and butter, so who am I to ask you to set a goal? Well, you've already bought the book so give it a go anyway.

PURE

Positive

It's easy to list what you don't want because your fear of failure will make you very well aware of the worst case scenario, and whilst it might seem that 'anything but that' is fine, it really isn't. While running away from danger you could fall off a cliff. Your brain is a system for minimising the gap between your dreams and reality, so focus on where you're going rather than what you're trying to avoid.

Under your control

You can't control your clients and your competitors. You can only control what you can touch. Focus only on the next action, the next step that you can take and the rest of the journey will follow.

Real

Your brain doesn't deal in the language of success and bank balances, it processes primary sensory information so present your goal in the language of your brain - what you can see, hear, feel and experience in your concrete, primary, first hand sensory experience. Success? What does it look like? Pro tip: Success is not found in what other people think of you.

Ecological

Every system operates in a complex balance, and if we change part of a system we risk upsetting that balance. The system will rebalance itself, but in a way which might not meet our individual needs. To recognise that you are part of a system, your goal must be ecological, preserving the balance of the world around you.

4.6.1   Your outcome

What is your outcome or goal as a salesperson?

4.7   Taming the Sales Monster

Ask your friends to describe a salesperson and they will probably say things like chatty, personable and success oriented. Ask people who aren't worried about hurting your feelings and they might say pushy, arrogant and flashy.

The biggest hurdle that you will ever have to get over in order to master sales is not tough clients, nor aggressive competitors, nor challenging market conditions. First, you have to tame the sales monster that lives inside you.

You had an experience of sales long before you got involved in sales for a living. You had experiences of being sold to, and you heard horror stories from other people about being sold to, ripped off, conned and so on. You heard from friends about dodgy cars, decrepit houses and all manner of things which did not live up to the expectations created by the sales person. 'Sales' became synonymous with 'untrustworthy'. Who would want to spend money with someone like that? If your mental image of a salesperson is of a pointy-haired, pointy-shoed, sharp-suited, fake-tanned smooth talker, or a big-haired, pointy-shoed, short-skirted, fake-tanned smooth talker, then you will try to prove that you are not that person. The more you try to prove it, the more you become that person, because that is your point of reference. Try as hard as you can not to be a sausage. Go on. Try really hard. You see? The harder you try not to be a sausage, the more you realise that you are, in fact, a sausage.

Your secret preconception of the worst type of salesperson is your own personal sales monster.

Monsters are entities that we never see or hear, yet we know they're real, because otherwise our fears would be irrational. We create monsters in order to explain why we avoid certain things, and make excuses for things we haven't done.

It's natural to fear rejection. It's natural to internalise a memory of someone else being rejected. We're a social species and our survival depends on acceptance. When we see someone being rejected, we quickly learn not to do what they did for fear of the same result. That's how we build monsters in our minds.

For you to be a naturally effective salesperson, you have to tame that monster, and the way to do that is to acknowledge its existence, and then to laugh in its face.

First, picture the person who you would hate to be seen as by your clients or friends. That's the monster. Then ask yourself, seriously, what is it that you are most afraid of, that the monster represents? Don't say 'nothing' because that's not normal. You're afraid of rejection, of not being liked, of not being good enough, of failure, of success, of being judged, of not being perfect, of being lost. You need approval, respect, trust, love. You need to be liked and cared for. And as a salesperson, you've thrown yourself into the job where you're most likely to have those fears provoked by rejection and the threat of failure, which will make you act out of insecurity and desperation, which will in turn alienate your clients and damage trust, which will reduce your success, which will make you act out of desperation, and so on.

All is not lost. When you acknowledge those fears, you own them, and when you own them, they can have no power over you.

Whenever you find yourself putting more energy into something than seems reasonable, or you find yourself putting something off that you really should get done, you are being motivated by fear. Acknowledge it, and then make a choice about your next action.

I know it's a cliché to say either do something or don't do it, however it really is true. Instead of having some sales actions sitting on your 'to do' list for weeks, acknowledge the fear that's keeping them there and either tackle them or discard them. It's your choice, no one is forcing you either way.

Remember that you'll only ever lose a client through lack of information, and your only barrier to being all that you want is yourself. The solution to both of those is simply to ask more questions.

The best sales people ask the questions that others are afraid to ask. The marketing gurus who bombard you with emails promising untold riches say that they ask the tough questions, but they really don't. They pretend to ask tough questions to push you into buying something that you're not sure about. That's a very different thing.

5: Products and Services

Are products and services the same? Do we sell them in the same way?

No. Definitely not. They are very different.

Let's first define what a service actually is:

> ## A service is an activity which adds value to a product

Here are a few examples.

Product	Service
Carpet	Fitting
Medical consumables	Application
Computers	Set-up
Books	Delivery
A business	Consultancy
A manager	Training
An employee	Coaching

I know. It's ridiculously simple.

What do we mean by "adds value"? Simply, that the service allows you to charge more for the product, and therefore makes it more valuable for the client because it saves them the time and cost and hassle of having to do something themselves. You could fit your own carpets and car tyres, or install your own computer software, or go and fetch your own books from the shop, but it's easier to pay someone else to do it.

When salespeople talk about "adding value", they really mean charging more money. However, the client won't pay more money for the same product, they expect something in return, and that's added value.

A service also enables you to differentiate a product from your competitors' offerings.

Consider these teapots. Which one would you buy?

Can't choose? OK, how about these three:

£9.95 plus £2 shipping	£11.95 with free shipping	£11.95 with free shipping and a free pack of tea

It's a simple example, right? You'll choose the teapot which has the highest perceived value, the one which gives you the most for your money.

You will have, no doubt, spotted an important point – that shipping and tea are not free. They have a cost.

Often, the cost of these types of services is hidden within the price of the product. We're so used to getting free delivery or fitting that most people wouldn't consider paying for the service, even if the overall cost was less.

Unless you are manufacturing something yourself which is in high demand relative to its supply, your margins on product sales will be low. Some retailers operate on a margin of around 1%. Computer distributors might get around 4%. If they sell a £1000 computer, they might retain £40 profit. How do they ever make a living?

You can see that, in a pure product sales business, you have to keep operating costs extremely low, and that often means that you end up cutting corners, which impacts on the client's perception of your products.

A product is a physical thing which is usually mass produced, or at least produced consistently. A customer can see a chair in a shop, order one, and the one that they get is the same as the one in the shop. If the customer doesn't like it, or if it's faulty, they can take it back. If the customer doesn't pay their bill, the supplier can take the product back.

A service is an intangible set of activities which ultimately add value to a product.

The single biggest problem with a service business is that you can't show the customer their product until after you have incurred the production costs, so the commercial risk is on you. Also, if the customer doesn't pay their bill, you can't take the service back, the customer has already benefited from it.

This presents two different challenges for service providers.

First, where the customer cannot do the job for themselves, you encounter the issue of their pride. For example, a lawyer, doctor or electrician might have technical skills that the client lacks, and so the client doesn't want to look stupid. The client wants to be kept informed, wants to be educated and wants to feel like they're part of the decision making process. The more the client trusts you, the more they will trust you to make decisions which are in their best interests, rather than expecting you to always recommend the most expensive option.

Secondly, where the customer chooses not to do the job for themselves, you encounter the issue of their expectations. For example, a client might hire a domestic cleaning service because they don't have time to do their own cleaning. Since they could do it themselves, they might have an expectation of how you should do it. The more the client trusts you, the more they will leave you to do it your way as long as the end result is what they had in mind.

Finding out what's in the client's mind is key to your success, and we'll come back to that later.

Services, when wrapped around products, protect margins and guard against simple price comparisons. The client is less likely to buy the cheapest because they can no longer compare like-for-like.

Some products are difficult to use without an element of service. Unless you're a trained carpet fitter or computer technician, you need someone else to make the product usable for you. Hence, what we often see in a retailer's advertising is:

Product	Service
Carpet	Free fitting
Computers	Free set-up
Books	Free next day delivery

We know that, in reality, those services are not free, we know that we pay a higher price for books and carpets in order to have them delivered and fitted. We have to take those costs into account when calculating our margins and hence our sales costs.

We could say that every business delivers an element of service, in that an activity has to take place to get the product to the client. Many companies train their staff to deliver good client service, however there is a problem with this...

> ## You can not provide good client service
>
> ## Good service is what the client experiences

As we'll see in a while, trying to deliver good client service can actually have a negative impact on your turnover.

There are many companies which focus more on services, or even completely on services.

An engineering company might offer design consultancy, installation and support, the value of which far outweighs that of the products sold.

A training or consultancy business might offer only services, with no tangible products changing hands. However, we can count knowledge, or Intellectual

Property, as a product in this case, because IP can be recorded in physical form, and it can be protected, and it can have a value on a company's balance sheet.

As a coach, you make use of intellectual property; knowledge, models, systems, methods and so on. How you use those to create value for your clients is unique to you.

We intuitively know that we like to visit shops that treat us well, however you can probably also think of instances where you've received outstanding service from a shop, restaurant or hotel, and you have never been back, perhaps because of its location or some other factor. You can perhaps also think of places where the service is just average, yet you go there regularly.

Service can be a differentiator, but if your client doesn't know that they're getting something special, they are unlikely to notice. All that you actually achieve is to reset their expectations at a higher level, so now you have to work even harder to keep them happy.

Retailers such as Amazon and eBay create a problem in the market. With next day, or even same day delivery, instant refunds, no-quibble returns and so on, these retailers don't just skew the client's expectations for their own businesses, they affect what a client expects from all businesses. When a corporate buyer gets next day delivery and an instant refund from Amazon for one book, he expects the same service when he's buying a multi-million pound computer network for his employer, too. Worse, he expects the same from you.

As a salesperson either selling a service, or using service as a differentiator, your biggest problem is that you think that good service increases profits, and that's not the case.

Research from the Association for Consumer Research on "Market Orientation and client Service" found a very strong connection between five links in the chain of events that connect service to profit:

However, other studies have found no significant connection between service and profit. Why?

The answer to this might be found in another research study from the University of Maryland, entitled, "Linkages between client service, client satisfaction and performance in the airline industry"

Quality of Customer Service

This research found that the connection between service and profit is 'non-linear', in other words, it's not a simple, direct connection, where more client service = more profit.

Better service leads to increased profits up to a certain point, and then it doesn't matter how much better your service is, your profits decline because the client doesn't care and the extra service costs money.

Buyers can only judge the quality of a product or service which is within their field of experience. Someone who has lived off fast food and ready meals for most of their life could appreciate that the food in a three Michelin starred restaurant is better, but they would be unlikely to get a job as a judge on MasterChef. To an uneducated client, a newly 'qualified' coach and a master coach with decades of experience would each do the same job. The client would not see why the master coach was charging more. Maybe the new coach would be operating at 90% of their capability, and the master coach would be operating at 10% but that's the point - both are more than capable. The client can't tell the difference.

You may have been seduced by social media marketing gurus who promise to help you sell 'high price coaching' and 'high ticket coaching' and 'high ticket coaching packages' and the like.

There is, of course, a contradiction within these claims. A Bentley car is not a 'high price' car. A Michelin starred restaurant is not a 'high price' restaurant. Both are appropriately priced for what you get, as is a small family car and a local cafe. If you can't tell the difference, if you think that "a car is a car, why pay more than you need to", then a Bentley is not for you.

If the gurus who are supposed to be teaching you how to sell think that your services are 'high priced' then what hope do you have?

High price is, of course, what the desperate coach wants. The social media gurus are exploiting the coach's need to make a living. High price. How to win clients without selling. These people might be making some money out of you, but you're not benefiting from the relationship. There are no quick wins, no get-rich-quick guarantees.

Deliver a high quality of service and set your prices appropriately to that. Yes, it's a long term strategy, but I promise you, it's the only sustainable strategy.

5.1　The Service Chain

To increase your profits through service, you have to understand how your own service chain links together, and in order to do that, you have to be able to measure activities.

5.1.1　The service chain

How can you measure performance in each of the five links in the service chain? Identify a measure and a suggestion for improvement for each.

Here's a simple example.

Client service

How many clients do you coach each week?

Client satisfaction

How many clients leave positive reviews?

Client retention

How many clients return or recommend you?

Sales growth

How much do those clients spend?

Profitability

What profit is achieved from that client spend?

The fundamental key to success in sales is **measurement**. If you can't measure it, then you can't track its impact on your turnover. If you're an employed salesperson on a guaranteed bonus in a big company, who cares? If you're self-employed then reducing your costs by removing non-essential activities is quite important, mostly because that then enables you to spend your time on activities which *do* increase your income.

Research in 2013 from the Miller Heiman Research Institute found that companies that measured client-focused behaviours had an average increase in profitability of 13% compared with other companies. This performance gap increased to 25% when combined with measurements of best practices in selling and sales management.

Examples of client-focused behaviours include:

- We use a formal process for measuring client satisfaction and loyalty

- Our salespeople have a solid understanding of our clients' business needs

- We clearly understand our clients' issues before we propose a solution

- We have relationships at the highest levels with all our most important accounts

- In an average week, our sales force spends sufficient time with clients

Let's put these three findings together.

Measuring client service behaviour › 13% increase in profit

Measuring client service and sales behaviour › 25% increase in profit

It's important to note that this is relative to the client's expectations of service. The 'optimum service level' depends on the company's brand image which in turn creates those client expectations. Clearly, Harrods' clients expect something different than Walmart's, but the same trade-off applies to both; once that optimum level is achieved, doing more for your clients adds no value, and may then be counter-productive.

The connection between client expectation and delivery could perhaps be summed up as follows:

> ## Your clients are happiest when you do what you say you're going to do

Why is there a connection between measuring activity and improving results?

Perhaps because, when you measure people doing the right things, they tend to do more of those things, because once they know they're being measured, they want to excel.

Measuring activity also allows you to **give feedback at the right time.**

If you want to know why you don't have enough clients, measure your activity, and you'll probably find that if you don't have enough clients today, you weren't talking to enough prospects a month ago.

What happens when you measure activity and give recognition for the right behaviours?

5.1.2   Your growth plans

Come up with some ideas for how you can make use
of these three pieces of research.

5.2   The Balance of Risk

In any sales transaction, there is a balance of risk
which shifts from one side to the other. Both the seller
and the buyer are happy when the risk is evenly shared
between both parties.

When you sell a physical product, the risk is that the
client won't be happy with it, for whatever reason.
They take a risk that they end up with a product which
isn't right for them, and you end up with their money
and won't give it back. Consumer laws protect the
buyer in such cases, and give the buyer confidence to
take the risk to buy your product. With any mass
produced product, the buyer can see an example so
that they know what to expect.

You can therefore choose a carpet, or a fitted kitchen,
or a new car based on your experience of the sample in
the showroom. If you're not happy with the specific
item that you receive, you return it and get a refund.

A seller cannot take a service back. You cannot unfit a
carpet or untrain a group of managers.

In a product sale, the risks balance out *before* the client
commits their hard earned cash, because they know
that they can return the product and get a refund.

In a service sale, the risks balance out *after* the client makes a commitment, which makes the salesperson's job more complicated. The client has to be certain that they're going to receive exactly what they hoped for.

You can therefore expect that, where a service has been applied to a product, such as fitting a carpet, you won't be able to return it because you don't like it, but only in the case of a fault such as damage to the carpet caused during either manufacture or fitting.

Of course, *every* product sale includes some element of a service, because consumer laws require consumer protection through warranties and returns.

The more that a service element makes up the package you're selling, the more risk there is on the buyer, because they don't really know what the service will be like until they've received it, and then it's too late to give it back for a refund.

Imagine you go to a restaurant. The descriptions in the menu sound great, but what the waiter delivers is way below your expectations. What do you do? In a worst-case scenario, you leave without paying and the restaurant loses a little bit of money from the ingredients but a lot more potential income from the time that you spent at the table, preventing another client from sitting there.

Highly commoditised 'fast food' outlets, which I can't bring myself to call 'restaurants', solve the problem by providing the exact same food, everywhere in the world, with handy pictures on the menu to show you what to expect.

There is still a margin of error, and you might still end up with something other than what you expected.

Here's a photo from such a menu:

And this is what I actually found in the box:

By the time I got home, I couldn't be bothered to go back and complain. I also didn't have any confidence that a replacement would be any better, and there we have the essence of the problem with service sales – confidence, also known as credibility.

What does credibility mean? It's the quality derived from the word credo, meaning 'I believe'. Confidence is the quality derived from the word confide, meaning to 'have trust'. Credibility and confidence both mean that the buyer believes that they will get what they expect from you.

With product sales, you don't need credibility as a salesperson, because the product is what it is, the client can look at it and fiddle with it, and if they don't like it they can give it back. They don't have to like you, and they don't have to trust you. In Jim Holden's model, you can be at level 1 and if the product is good, you'll do OK.

With service sales, your credibility is everything. If the client doesn't trust and believe you, they will project that lack of confidence onto the service. It doesn't matter how many years of experience your engineers have between them, or how many accreditations your service desk has, or what your testimonials say, if the client doesn't believe you, it's game over.

When you are both the salesperson and the service provider, you can see that credibility becomes even more important, because the client can't tell where one role ends and the other begins.

Building trust is the subject of endless books and articles from gurus who advocate team building exercises, showing integrity, finding win-win outcomes, making eye contact and using an up-to-date social media profile photo.

Trust is automatic. All you have to do to maintain it is do what you say you're going to do. Whether that's sending an email, calling when you say you will, sending the information that you promised, what you do creates an expectation of what your service will do.

5.3   Differentiation

You've probably come across the importance of differentiating your services. As a result, you have probably, at some point, considered what kind of a coach, trainer or consultant you are. You might have considered calling yourself a life coach, or a wellness coach, or a career coach, or a life empowerment transformation breakthrough coach, or similar.

If your prospect says, "Eh? What?" then your title is making you stand out, but for the wrong reasons.

All job titles are relational. Job titles do not describe what you do, they describe who you are from the point of view of your clients. Make your title easy for them to understand. Don't worry about trying to sound and look different to your competitors because you already do, there is only one of you.

Differentiation does not mean being better, it means being different, which enables a prospect to more easily choose between options. Think about the teapots. They were undifferentiated, so you had to look for some other criteria upon which to base your decision. Similarly, if a prospect is looking at three coaches, and all have the same qualifications, and all call themselves a wellness breakthrough life transformation coach, and all are the same price, how does the prospect choose which to work with?

The answer is that they will choose the one they like. That could be the one the relate to, or the one they like the look of, or the one who was born in the same town, or the one who also loves a certain brand of coffee. Who knows? The point is that the prospect will *always* make a subjective decision, whether you consciously differentiate your service or not.

Differentiation makes the prospect's decision easier because it puts the points of reference further apart. This could just as easily make the prospect choose someone else instead of you. I think that a lot of 'sales experts' talk about points of differentiation as if they are the things you do to make a prospect more likely to buy. This is not true, and it's not useful either. When a service is more clearly differentiated, the prospect's decision will be easier and faster. It could go your way, and it could just as easily go the other way.

Differentiation is an intrinsic part of qualification. You might see a trend amongst lifestyle gurus that they tell you why they *don't* want you as a client. I've seen mock webinars where the guru says, "Don't sign up for the consultation if you don't have the money to invest, and you're not ready to take massive action, because I don't want to work with you". It's all part of a hard sell. If you wanted hard sell tactics, or if you believed that they lead to good relationships, you wouldn't be reading this book. You know there are no 'quick wins'.

6:   Selling Yourself

If you're a service provider of any kind then at some point I'm sure you've come across the problem of selling yourself, or selling your time. Maybe you've found it difficult to convince someone of the need for your services. Maybe you've found it difficult to defend your rates.

The good news is that you don't have to sell yourself, because there's only one of you, so you wouldn't get very far with that.

The other good news is that you don't have to sell your time. Your client has the same amount of time as you, so they don't need your time and they're unlikely to pay for it, unless they're being greedy.

The bad news is that if you can't sell yourself, and you can't sell your time, you have to figure out exactly what it is that you are selling.

If you try to apply product sales techniques to a service, you will most likely end up doing what most service providers do – giving away a 'free consultation' or a 'free exploratory coaching session'. The client isn't fooled – they know that it isn't free. They know that they will have to pay for your time in two ways.

Firstly, the client will have to pay by giving you information, and you will use that information to sell more of your services to them. The client knows that their information is valuable, because you are willing to give your time to get it.

You'll find the take-up of these free consultations to be less than you expected, because the other important thing to understand is that the client is paying with their time, and their time is the most valuable thing they have. Once they've given you their time, they can never get that back.

That simple idea is the basis for understanding how to sell your services.

I have heard so many independent service providers saying, "I don't like selling myself" and as I said before, you can't sell yourself, you are not a slave. Of course, they're not really talking about selling themselves, they are talking about being personally judged for doing a bad job. There is a very simple solution to this problem. Don't do a bad job. There, all sorted.

What about people who have made some kind of career change and don't think anyone will believe them? Some people call this 'imposter syndrome' but let's not get into that, because I don't even believe that it exists. Don't start citing academic research at me, because if I can get 500 people to say that, yes, sometimes they do wonder if we're all living inside a big computer simulation then I could call it simulation syndrome and win a Nobel prize or something.

Let's apply Occam's Razor. Is there likely to be a neurological condition in which a person's senses create an illusion of being underqualified for a job? Or is it more likely that the person actually really is underqualified for the job, but nobody notices because nobody cares and almost everybody is underqualified for their jobs because you can't get qualifications in most of what people do in the course of their jobs.

"But that's not what I meant. I mean, like, if I'm talking to a prospect and they're asking me about my coaching experience, I feel like I don't have enough experience and I can't justify what I'm saying to them."

Well, that's a good example of not having enough experience, and only being able to explain something in terms that were given to you by someone else. So if there is such a thing as Imposter Syndrome, this is it. You are pretending to be someone else. You are trying to explain the power of coaching using the words given to you on your coaching training course. That's the essence of the problem. You don't actually know how to explain the power of coaching in your own words. Experience will solve this problem. Getting experience involves making a lot of mistakes but if you are open to that then you will learn fast and achieve success more quickly.

It's not all your fault. The big coach training companies, who pretend to be professional bodies but aren't, are making the problem worse by giving coaches sales scripts which just don't work. They can't work, unless you give the prospect the other half of the script so that they know their lines too.

If sales scripts worked then every salesperson would be a millionaire and every buyer would be defenceless against their hypnotic power.

Is Imposter Syndrome a psychological problem? This is like saying that your computer just doesn't do video editing. It just doesn't. It can't. You know that it isn't the computer that's the problem, you just haven't installed the right software. In fact, your computer can do anything that you might want it to do, but not fresh out of the box. You upgrade your computer hardware from time to time, but your human hardware has a lifetime warranty, and we all have the same hardware. To do anything useful, your computer has to learn. The same goes for you.

What we're really talking about here is credibility. Coaches, consultants, lawyers, all kinds of experts worry about building their credibility.

Unfortunately, you have none. And you will never have any credibility.

The reason for this is not because of your lack of experience or qualifications. It is simply because credibility is a quality which you can never have. Why would I say such an outrageous and obviously true thing? Well, the word 'credibility' comes from the Latin 'credo', meaning 'I believe'. To believe is an action performed by one person to another person or object or concept.

Credibility is not what you have, it is what your prospects have, or more accurately, it is the quality that your prospects project onto you. We know that con men, since the time the first caveman sold a dodgy wheel to a caveman from another tribe, have learned to emulate the short cuts that we take when evaluating whether to believe someone.

Everyone who has ever been conned out of their life savings has said, "But he was so believable, he was smart and drove a nice car and had a brief case and everything". Well, of course. Humans, like many animals, are great mimics.

FOR SALE

GOOD RUNNER. RECENT MOT.

CLEAN. ONE CAVELADY OWNER.

SOLD AS SEEN.

Every sale is an exchange of equal value.

Any currency in the world is based on trust. We tend to trust a government issued bank note more than an IOU note, although that depends on who wrote it, and the government in question.

The more you trust in the value of a currency, the more it is worth on the exchange markets. The market values fluctuate because the amount of trust changes. When a government announces a new policy, it impacts on trust. Recessions are a breakdown of trust.

The value of your services is equally based on trust, or we might call it credibility. The more you have, the more your services are worth.

But where does credibility come from?

You can't tell people that you're credible. Even telling people about all your accomplishments doesn't build credibility, because no-one ever willingly displayed a testimonial from an unhappy customer. That's why comparison and review sites became popular, however once their owners turn them into marketing channels, they lose their credibility again.

The key here is vested interest. If someone recommends you, they need to have nothing to gain, only the pleasure of passing on good news. The client knows that you gain from testimonials, and that reduces their credibility. They're not without value, but they are one part of a bigger picture.

Many people leave the corporate world to start their own business and wonder why they've lost their credibility, just because the name on their business card has changed. The answer is that they never had any, they were borrowing the credibility of their employer.

Qualifications are another way of implying credibility, and the greater the credibility of the school or university, the more the qualification is worth.

You might also build credibility through:

- Referrals

- Social media

- Books

- Consistency

Everything that you post on social media is visible to the world, and you can expect clients to check up on you to see if you're what you seem to be.

Everything that you write on your website, in an email, on social media is a positioning statement. It isn't true, it's what you want people to know about you. The name of your business, your job title, these are also positioning statements.

There are two very important things that you have to bear in mind.

Firstly, your positioning statements have to be true for you. They have to be what you want to do, not what you think your clients want to hear.

Secondly, your statements have to be consistent.

You know that we communicate over many different channels, with the content of our language making up only part of the meaning that the listener takes away. Some people argue about the percentages; what's important is that words have little meaning without context, part of which is non-verbal. The more those channels are aligned, the greater the impact of what you're communicating.

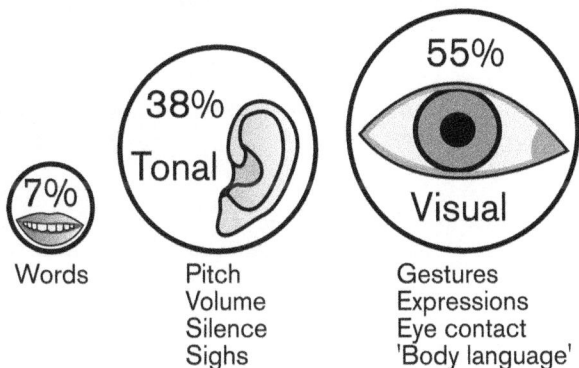

Words	Pitch	Gestures
	Volume	Expressions
	Silence	Eye contact
	Sighs	'Body language'

In fact, the alignment between these channels is the primary way that we decide if someone is telling the truth. Inconsistency is confusing. Your client won't take the time to wonder why you're being inconsistent, they'll simply stop listening to you. They'll stop believing you. And you will have lost your credibility.

The simplest way to ensure consistency is, as I said, to say what is true for you. When you think about describing your services, focus on what you want, what you're interested in, what you enjoy doing. Forget your clients for now. When you're focused on what's right for you, your communication will be consistent and you'll attract the clients that are right for you.

When I say 'attract', I don't mean that clients will magically find you, I mean that your consistent marketing and sales communication will get the attention of the right clients, and the wrong clients will tend to ignore it.

For example, if you mention your fees up front, you will tend to push away the people who think they can get your services for free, which saves your time.

Anything that saves you time in the sales process means that you can devote more time to what really works for you.

7:   Types of Sales

Most peoples' experience of sales comes from being on the receiving end of consumer or 'B2C' sales. When a business sells to another business, that's called B2B sales.

It's worth understanding different sales models because there are many different ways that you will sell your services, not only direct to clients but through other intermediaries such as employers or agencies. If you understand how to 'sell through' as well as 'sell to' then you will have many more options for developing your business and ensuring sustainable success. I suspect that there are hardly any coaches who make a comfortable living from only one type of sales relationship.

You've probably read of the promise of 'passive income' from books, online courses and other similar information products. I'm sorry to have to tell you that no income is passive. You have to work for every penny you earn. The only difference is whether you are directly charging for your time or not, and if you can understand the different sales relationships within a supply chain then you have a much better chance of adjusting your approach to match different products and services that are part of your business plan.

It's easy for coaches to focus on the coaching interaction itself, and forget about the complexity of the sales interaction, so let's look at some examples.

7.1   The Supply Chain

We generally only think in terms of a salesperson selling to a user, however this is almost never the case. Most of the time, a number of transactions take place in a sequence called a 'supply chain'.

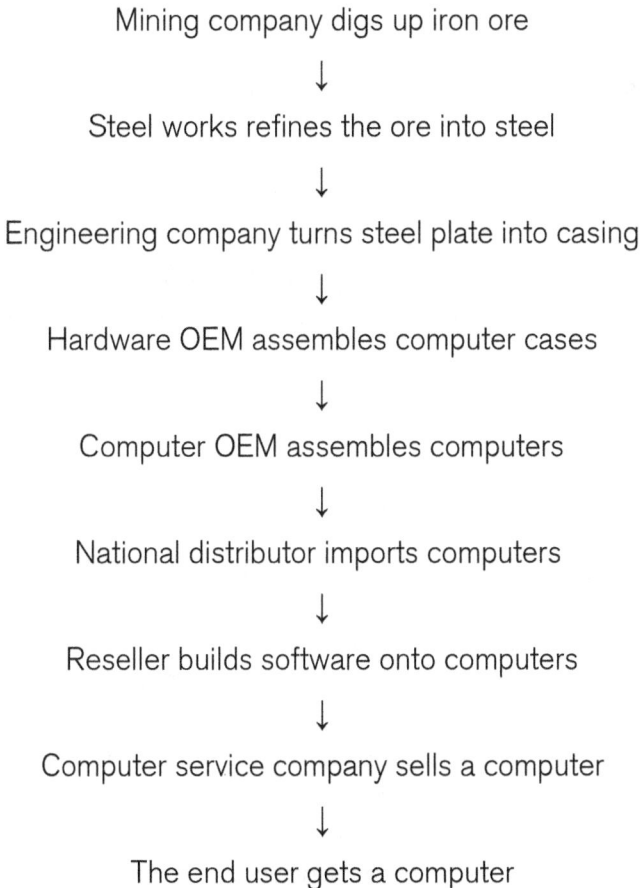

Mining company digs up iron ore

↓

Steel works refines the ore into steel

↓

Engineering company turns steel plate into casing

↓

Hardware OEM assembles computer cases

↓

Computer OEM assembles computers

↓

National distributor imports computers

↓

Reseller builds software onto computers

↓

Computer service company sells a computer

↓

The end user gets a computer

We haven't even looked at the supply chain involving the user of the computer yet! Each of these links needs sales people and buyers to manage the sequence of processes.

Direct selling is generally regarded as selling to the end user, and indirect is where we're selling to someone who then sells to an end user. In reality, the transactions within a business don't form a neat 'supply chain' because many different products and services come together to serve many different clients.

If you own a grocery shop, is the person who comes in to buy a bag of flour the end user? Or is it the person they're baking the birthday cake for? Or is it the guests at the birthday party?

Some companies have two types of salespeople, one team sells to a corporate buyer, the other tries to influence the end user. This is known as 'pull-through' selling or 'demand creation'.

Indirect sales team → **client** ← Demand creation team

In this instance, the client is typically a buyer in a reseller company, such as a retailer or wholesaler. Sales people go and pitch to the buyers, and of course the buyers could choose from many similar products to serve their own clients. By creating demand, the demand creation sales team gives the buyer an incentive to select their products, because the buyer knows that clients will already be interested.

Usually, the job of demand creation is done through general marketing and advertising. The difference with a demand creation sales team is that they will speak to a specific client about buying specific products, and then allow that client to choose the best reseller to get those products from. With marketing, you can't really see who is looking at your adverts and leaflets, and you don't know which of your competitors they're also looking at. Social media marketing does of course enable you to track engagement.

The answer to the question of who is the end user or client in your grocery shop is easy to understand when you think about what a bag of flour actually is. It is a bag of flour. A bag, containing flour. That's it.

Therefore, the person who comes in to buy it is the end user, because when they get home and bake the birthday cake, the flour is no longer flour, it is now a cake. The end user is the person who consumes the product or service. Anyone else, such as the guests at the birthday party, is a **stakeholder**. Not a direct decision maker, but perhaps an **influencer**.

7.2   Inbound and Outbound

We also have to consider the direction of the sales relationship. This usually refers to the first contact with a potential client, so if you're calling them, that's an outbound call, and if they're calling you, that's an inbound call. You need to handle them differently.

The important point to remember here is that when the client calls you, they are not having their first experience with you. They are calling because they have seen or read something, or spoken to someone, and they therefore have expectations.

Many sales people treat an inbound call as an enquiry but it is not - it is a response to something you've previously done. This applies for all inbound contacts, whether by phone, email or social media.

If you have multiple 'shop windows' where the caller might have found your details, you can see that the first fact for you to establish is what they are calling in response to. Only then will you know the context for the call and the appropriate response. Otherwise, they are already half way through their conversation with you when you drag them back to the start and ask them to explain it all over again.

No doubt you've had the experience of having to explain your problem over and over again as you were passed from person to person in a call centre. Your prospective client feels the same way when you ask them to start from the beginning.

The most important thing with this first contact situation is to take control of the conversation. You might think that when you make the call, you're already in control, but that's not the case. The prospective client will quite easily take control if you're not prepared.

How to Sell Coaching

Once we get into the sales cycle itself, in the Opening section, I'll explain a very easy way for you to take control of the conversation without the prospect feeling pushed or pulled. For now I'll give you a clue to ponder on: The person who is in control of the conversation is the person asking questions.

7.3   Direct and Indirect

With direct selling, the person who buys the product or service is the person who will use it for its primary purpose.

With indirect selling, the person who buys the product or service is doing so because of its added value, not because of its primary purpose.

You → Channel → End user

You → End user

Imagine you have a small engineering company.

A classic car enthusiast might buy a part from you to restore a car. He is the client, the buyer, the decision maker and the user.

A maintenance company might buy a part from you to repair a client's machine. The end user doesn't know who supplied the part. The added value is that the part you supply enables your client to repair something for their client.

A company that stocks parts for classic cars might order a batch of a particular part from you so that they can supply their clients, who might be either car owners or car parts retailers. The added value is that they have the part in stock, so it's available immediately for clients.

Therefore the real value of a product or service is the cost plus the value to the client, and each client will perceive value differently.

The larger the client's business, the more likely they are to have professional buyers who manage supplier relationships to deliver best value, which generally means getting the best product and the best service at the best price.

The important point to take from this is that you need to know who you are selling to, because the person who you're talking to might be a decision maker, end user or recommender, or all three.

7.3.1   Who is the client?

Can you think of some examples?

Think of some different sales relationships and identify the:

- Decision Maker

- Recommender

- End User

7.4   Why Should I Care?

As I've mentioned before, you've bought the book now so you might as well get your money's worth.

Also, we might consider some parallels between direct and indirect selling in the 'real world' and selling your services as a coach.

Direct

Direct selling puts the salesperson in direct contact with the end user. In coaching, this means that you, the coach, is talking to the client directly. They are the buyer, the decision maker and the end user all rolled into one. This might sound like the ideal situation, but it really isn't. This client is unlikely to be an expert in buying. They will tend to buy from someone they like rather than someone who can do the job. They will base their decision on subjective impressions rather than objective criteria. They won't care about your certificates or expensive training.

Even when selling direct, you still need to think about the role of influencers, people who are not directly responsible for the decision but who will still think it necessary to stick their oar in and kick the tyres. Automotive salespeople are now trained to ask who else the prospect might need to talk to in order to feel comfortable with their decision, rather than just getting annoyed when the prospect says, "I don't know, I need to talk to my wife/husband/friend who knows about these things".

Indirect

Indirect selling puts the salesperson in contact with a buyer who is a different person to the end user. The buyer has their criteria which would incorporate the needs of the end user too. In coaching, this means that you're selling the quality and credibility of your service to a buyer such as a HR manager who is choosing you for reasons other than you being the most amazing coach ever. They need to be able to justify their decision, so they might well ask about your certificates and training, if they have experience of buying coaching services. They might also be looking for criteria such as scalability, which is your ability to meet their increasing demand for your time. Large corporate buyers will be more likely to buy from corporate coaching providers because if a coach calls in sick, a replacement will be sent. You might think that this isn't right, because the coach is special and unique. The coach provides a service, and anyone with the same certificates can provide that service.

Another indirect contact might be a line manager who wants to buy coaching for someone in their team. Be careful of managers with a remedial focus who give you instructions for how to coach their staff, and what they want you to get their staff to do better. The risk here is the alignment of expectations. The manager and the end user could have very different ideas of what is needed!

Even when you think you're selling direct, other people may be involved because the end user isn't able or willing to take full responsibility for their decision. You'll hear, "I don't know, I need to talk to my wife/husband/friend who knows about these things". This *could* be a disguised stall, because they're just not happy with what you've said but they don't want to say that, or it could mean that they like to get a second opinion on important decisions, or it could mean that they are able to make decisions, but fear that this other person will then say, "You bought WHAT???"

Their reasons for delaying the decision may well relate to what they want to get out of the coaching process, so this is a rare example where you could shift from your sales brain into your coaching brain.

Traditional sales techniques would have you challenge the prospect and put them on the spot to make a decision, and they might then do that, but could just as easily undecide later on when they no longer feel under pressure from you. I would therefore suggest that you focus on reassurance and then wait patiently. If their wife/husband/friend is able to derail the decision, they would likely derail the coaching process anyway.

The simple approach is to treat this as an indirect sell.

If you're selling indirectly to a single decision maker who is more concerned with you as an individual than with scalability, you're probably speaking to a manager in a small business. The most important thing to remember is that the buyer's reasons for buying will not be the same as those for the end user, and so you have to uncover both sets of needs.

Wholesale

Selling to wholesale means that someone thinks your product or service would be of interest to their customers, but they don't have any specific customer in mind. They're happy to list your product for sale, because if it doesn't sell, the risk is on you. In coaching, this would be something like an agency or directory which is happy to list your coaching service without any specific referral and without any expectation that you'll actually sell any coaching.

Wholesale channels are generally easy to get into, because they're taking almost no risk. The downside is that all of your competitors will be there too.

Associate relationships can work like wholesale sales channels, where the client facing brand is happy to listen anyone as an associate in the hope that it makes them look bigger and more credible. It doesn't, and it doesn't help you either.

Reseller

A reseller chooses to sell a specific product to specific buyers because they believe that it fits with their overall business plan and adds to their credibility. For example, if you're looking for a camera and you go to one of the big high street chains, you'll find the don't stock every brand. They have reseller relationships with brands which they know will be popular, and they often have exclusive rights to sell specific model variations, or early access to new models. When you see adverts for new smartphones, you'll often see that they are exclusive to a particular network for a period of time.

Referrals are essentially reseller sales. The clients or contacts who refer you to their friends and colleagues are not referring every coach they have ever spoken to. They are making a specific referral because they believe that you will add value to their network.

Associate relationships can work like reseller channels, where the client facing brand is using only selected coaches to supply a service on their behalf. They will usually do this because taking on employees is expensive and risky. If they run short of client work, the risk is on you, not them.

Integration

A systems integrator will put together a bespoke solution for a client's problem which combines multiple products and services from multiple vendors. IBM used to make computers, now they're almost exclusively an integrator. The solution is always a perfect fit for the client, but it requires a different style of selling known, oddly enough, as 'solution selling'.

Everyone from a double glazing salesperson to the assistant in a shoe shop will try to convince you that they are offering you a 'solution'. This is not true. They are offering you a commodity product which broadly meets your needs. They just think that 'solution' sounds better.

Solution selling is bespoke, the relationship is normally at a high decision making level and the criteria are financial, hence one of the hallmarks of a solution sales process is that the solution presentation uses a 'value proposition', which basically goes like this: Our solution will save you £1m a year for a one-off capital cost of £1.2m with a lifespan of 5 years".

A value proposition creates a short cut for the decision making process. In the old days, a sales person would meet the buyer's technical needs and then the buyer would have to make an internal business case to raise the funding. The value proposition goes straight to the business case.

An integration sales process normally means that the sales team working at the client interface are the only people who communicate with the client, and everyone vendor who is providing part of the overall solution is only ever in the background, they have no direct client contact.

In coaching, if a large learning and development services provider won a contract to supply coaches to a large organisation, they would recruit and train associates to work under a 'white label', in other words, to represent the L&D company and not promote their own services directly. If you were working as an associate in such a way and you gave a client one of your own business cards, you could be sure to see the end of that working relationship very quickly. Protecting the L&D provider's brand and client relationship is paramount.

7.5   Protecting Your Channel

The channel, remember, is your route to market. The challenge and cost of scaling your marketing activities mean that you're unlikely to make a comfortable full time living by only selling direct to end users. It's more likely that your income will be a mix of your own clients and those who you're working with through indirect channels to market - associate work, in other words.

Independent coaches, trainers and consultants often get themselves into a cycle of events which is ultimately counter productive and even self destructive. Here's how it goes.

- The coach is short of work and looks for companies hiring associates

- The coach is successful in getting selected as an associate

- The coach finds out how much the client is paying relative to how much the coach is getting paid

- The coach offers to work with the client direct and cut out the 'middle man'

- The associate work ends abruptly

- Repeat

The root cause of this cycle of events is that the coach has no experience of sales and marketing and thinks that the contract owner is doing nothing for their cut. The coach has no idea how much work goes into winning the contract, and so attributes no value to it. Over time, it gets harder and harder for the coach to re-enter the world of associate work. Word gets around. It's a small industry.

If the coach gets lucky, the cycle goes like this:

- The coach is short of work and looks for companies hiring associates

- The coach is successful in getting selected as an associate

- The coach finds out how much the client is paying relative to how much the coach is getting paid

- The coach offers to work with the client direct and cut out the 'middle man'

- The coach works with that client for a while, but when the work dries up, the coach has no idea how to find more

- Repeat

This variation has the same root cause. The coach doesn't value the work done and, most importantly, the risk taken by the contracting company. There's a saying in the recruitment industry and I think it actually applies to freelance coaching, training and consulting too - "You either do it for six months or you do it forever". Six months is the time it takes for a new recruiter to find jobs for all their friends. Six months is the time it takes for all the coaching referrals from your friends and old colleagues to run out. After that, if you don't develop your sales skills, you'll be trying to get back into full time employment.

If you are ever going to consider associate work then there are some rules which you must keep in mind to protect trust and credibility within your working relationship. I do know some coaches, trainers and consultants who work exclusively as associates for a number of different contracting companies. They don't earn as much per day as they would if they worked directly, but they value the fact that they don't have to spend any time on marketing and sales. However, they also understand the importance of developing and protecting those associate relationships.

Here are the rules.

- See yourself as a custodian of the brand of the contracting company, their employee, their representative, their ambassador

- Never communicate directly with the end user about the contract, pricing etc.

- Never give the end user your own branded business card or contact details (unless the contracting company tells you to)

- If you hear any complaints about the service provision, tell your contact in the contracting company

- If you discover any competitor activity in the client's business, such as names in the visitor book, tell your contact in the contracting company

- If the end user asks you any questions about changes or additions to the service, don't refer them to the contracting company, connect them personally for an opportunity to demonstrate your loyalty

- Be loyal, responsive and easy to work with

- Never forget that selling the service is the hard, risky part, and delivering the service is the easy, safe part

You can see that what you have to do to protect your associate relationship is much the same as you would do in any relationship. Be honest and loyal.

It's very easy, when working as an associate, to 'go native' and lose yourself in the end user's organisation, forgetting that you are the trusted representative of the contracting company.

Perhaps the most common complaint that associates have is that the contracting companies have too many associates and don't guarantee enough work, so the associate has no choice but to find other associate relationships or direct client work.

Perhaps the most common complaint that contracting companies have is that their associates don't guarantee availability, so the company has no choice but to find more associates so as to maintain client service.

Both the associate and the contracting company are trying to reduce the risk of unavailability, which is often what causes the problem in the first place. The reality is that contracting companies often use associates because they don't have enough work to justify employing coaches, so there's unlikely to be enough work for the coach to pay their bills anyway.

If the company employed coaches full time, they would have an incentive to fully utilise those people. However, if their volume of business doesn't warrant the risk of hiring employees, they will use freelance contractors in the knowledge that they can take a few hours here and there, not caring how the associate is going to live on such a small income, and not caring that the associate may then be forced back into a full time job because there's always another associate knocking at the door, looking for work.

This low-commitment attitude is what causes associates to find other income sources. By failing to give commitment, the company doesn't get commitment.

I go to Hong Kong twice a year and deliver a training program through a training centre there. We have a mutually exclusive agreement, I don't train the subject with anyone else in Hong Kong, and they don't have any other trainer for the subject than me. They handle all of the marketing and hosting, I turn up, do my thing, get paid. If any of their clients want private coaching sessions in between trips, I pay them a referral fee for the first three sessions. Just last night, a client who I had two private sessions with in Hong Kong contacted me and asked for a follow up. She said that she wanted to deal with me directly. As tempting as it is to keep all of the fee for myself, what I have to weigh up is the relative value of these two relationships. One client, one session, maybe a handful of sessions, versus two training programs per year, plus other webinars, plus private sessions, plus book sales, plus who knows what in the future as their business grows and diversifies. The owner of the centre values commitment above all else, because she wants to be able to make solid commitments to the clients who come into her centre to access a range of services from different providers.

Another common problem is that the sales person in the contracting company thinks that saying 'yes' is what their clients want. They manage to sell a coaching service and tell the client that they'll have a team there first thing on Monday, even though the client didn't ask for it. Then they'll round up whoever is available because they think that being available and responsive is better than being good.

I'm sure you'll remember the relationship between quality of service and profit, in that better service does indeed increase profits. The problem here is that the sales person doesn't know what 'better service' actually entails for that client. Their attitude to business is one of a low value wholesaler, many of whom base their business philosophy on that of Harry Gordon Selfridge, which to paraphrase is "If you ain't got it, you can't sell it". You'll recognise this as a philosophy which treats the associate as a commodity; readily available, interchangeable and where low cost is the selection criteria.

You'll also recall this graph:

Quality of Customer Service

Providing 'quality' without qualifying what the client actually wants and values will result in declining profits.

I know of a training company which is reasonably successful and which has built its business on the exploitation of associates. Their approach borders on modern slavery. Here's what happens, and perhaps you will recognise some of these behaviours from companies you've worked with.

The training company spends tens of thousands of Pounds every month on advertising. If you search the internet for various types of 'off the shelf' corporate training, you'll probably see their adverts. A prospective client will then send an enquiry and within an hour will have a proposal that seems tailored just to them. When the client buys a day's training at £1250, the sales person then emails the pool of associates. The first one to reply gets the work. We could be cruel and say that if an associate is usually available for work then they're not very busy, and not very good.

Associates are paid around £250 to £400 which includes the day's work and all of the design of the workshop and the production of materials, and usually travel expenses too. If the associate spends a day designing and writing a workshop, their effective day rate has become £125 to £200.

The training company keeps the associate's materials and materials. Strangely, when another request for exactly the same training comes in again, they will get another associate to design their own workshop rather than reuse the materials they already have.

Quality is not the training company's success criteria. The owner of the company started the business by seeing how much corporate trainers were charging and realising he could sell associates at a far higher price than they were prepared to work for if he 'wowed' the client with a jazzy proposal and slick presentation. Their target client is therefore a training manager or small business owner who doesn't know how to assess the quality of learning and who thinks that training is all the same. The training company is almost never successful in selling to professional L&D managers.

The associates who are delivering training for this company for maybe 2 or 3 days every week are happy. They know they could make more money by selling direct, but they could never compete with the training company's advertising spend which is specifically targeting buyers who don't understand or want quality, they just want a training course.

The associates who only get a handful of days' work will quickly move on somewhere else.

Everyone wants loyalty, but it comes at a cost.

8:   The Sales Cycle

Why do we say that sales is a cycle?

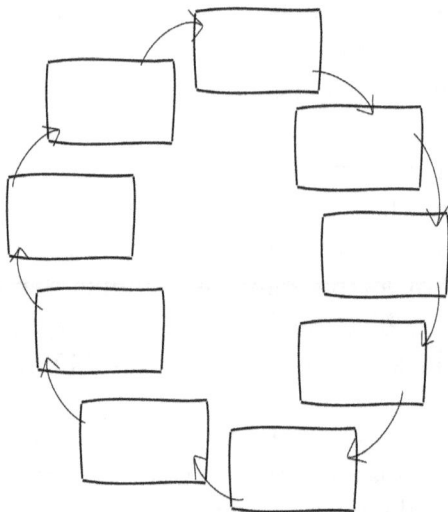

Because we want our clients' repeat business. It's much cheaper to acquire than new business, and it stops your competitors from gaining an advantage in your market. Every order that a client places with you is a new sales lead. On the other hand, every one of your current clients is a potential new client for your competitors, and in general, sales people are more driven to win new business than to farm their existing contacts. Maybe it's the thrill of the chase, who knows?

In the 1980s, Jim Holden developed a new approach to selling, and in the book that went with it (Power Base Selling), he defined four types or levels of salesperson.

Level 1

Focuses on: Not being rejected

Behaviour: Happy if a client engages in a conversation

Prospects: New

Level 2

Focuses on: Closing the sale

Behaviour: Qualifies hard and pushes to close the deal

Prospects: New

Level 3

Focuses on: Generating repeat sales

Behaviour: Gets to know the buying process

Prospects: Existing

Level 4

Focuses on: Building a relationship

Behaviour: Gets to know the client and their business

Prospects: Existing

Sales people operating at levels 1 and 2 tend to focus on new leads and don't revisit existing clients. Sales people operating at levels 3 and 4 tend to focus on 'farming' existing clients and sometimes shy away from generating new prospects. So other than level 1, it isn't a case of which approach is best, it's a case of matching the sales approach to the client.

For example a corporate buyer for a large systems integrator will have many potential requirements and a level 3 salesperson is a good match; understanding the procurement process, getting to know the influencers, using the client's language etc.

However, a smaller company where you're dealing with an end user is more likely to be a good match for a level 2 salesperson who pushes for the order and then moves on to the next lead. A level 2 salesperson might be pushy, they might be very tactful and patient. Their personality and their working environment don't change their focus on winning an order.

Even a level 1 salesperson will win orders, but he or she is unlikely to be in control of the conversation, and their performance will be unpredictable. The main reason that we measure so much in sales is that we try to predict what our sales performance is going to be.

It's easy to think that we want salespeople to sell as much as possible, and this is a mistake that small businesses often make. What we really want is for salespeople to sell exactly as much as we want them to so that we can plan our business resources accordingly.

If we give salespeople uncapped bonuses, the best ones will figure out the quickest way to sell over their targets to earn as much money as possible. They might then create problems with delivery, because you don't have enough stock, or engineers, or enough money in the bank to buy the stock and pay the engineers.

Cashflow is a very important issue for any business. Whatever you do for a living, you understand cashflow. You know that you can't go to the pub until after payday. You could probably buy a new carpet on credit, which means you would pay more for it in the long run. When cashflow is limited to the cash in your pocket, it's easy to manage how much you can spend on a night out and still have enough money for a taxi home, or you could have a few more drinks and get the bus home. Or you could have a few more drinks and forget where you live anyway.

Let's assume that you close a massive deal today for some computer hardware, a project which will take 6 months to implement. The client signs the contract but won't pay anything until after they have accepted the completion of the project. In order to implement the project, your company has to buy the computer equipment and pay the people who will install it. Meanwhile, you have been paid your handsome bonus and are sunning it up in some all inclusive resort in the Caribbean. Half way through the project, your company runs out of cash and ceases to exist.

There are several problems with this. Your company should have:

- Set your target to act as a disincentive to winning such a big project

- Not paid your bonus until the project was completed, giving you an incentive to manage the client relationship

- Negotiated a staged payments plan with the client to cover the up-front costs

- Negotiated longer payment terms with the computer hardware manufacturer

That's good in hindsight. I'm sure you'll find yourself another good sales job anyway. After all, everyone wants to hire a salesperson who smashes their targets.

Usually, sales people don't have to worry about things like this. It's someone else's problem to set their target and bonus system correctly and manage the resources of the business.

Once salespeople think about the wider impact of their activities, they move up those Holden levels.

As a self employed coach, trainer or consultant, you don't have to worry about bonuses and profits, because all of your income is rolled into one lump. Similarly, you probably roll all of your outgoings into one lump as well. You might want to think about cashflow more carefully if you're the kind of person who occasionally looks at your bank balance and has only one of two reactions:

- Enough - I can go on a spending spree

- Not enough - panic, find some clients

You might consider your income as being split into two parts, as if you were employed as a sales person.

The first part is your 'basic'. That's the minimum you're guaranteed to earn each month.

The second part is your 'bonus'. That's what you get as an incentive for hitting your targets.

When I'm working on a large project, I promise myself a reward if I win it, such as a new gadget, something which on an ordinary day I wouldn't justify buying for myself. I find that it helps to keep me focused on what I need to do to win the project. You might find that this works for you, or that something else does. But do find something that works.

You can easily calculate your basic monthly outgoings, the absolute minimum that you have to earn. Remember to factor in tax, otherwise your tax bill comes as a nasty surprise at the end of the year!

You should also calculate what it costs you to sell your services. This is known as 'cost of sale' and there is even a box for this on your annual tax return. Cost of sale is advertising, marketing, travel expenses, business cards, electricity, your web site and domain name, all of the running costs of your business. Again, you can easily calculate what these are by looking at your bank and credit card statements.

So now we have three levels of income:

Bonus: Covers your treats, holidays, nights out

Business: Covers your essential operating costs

Basic: Covers your essential living costs

As we progress through the sales cycle, you will see how to calculate your 'conversion rate' so that you know what marketing and sales activities are the most reliable ways to generate new client income, and also what it costs you to secure a new client relationship.

8.1   The Buying Process

When anyone makes a buying decision, they follow a consistent process:

Information

Finding out about what is available, potential suppliers

Decision

Narrowing down choices, making a decision

Buying

Buying the product, asking about credit, delivery, warranty etc.

Owning

Taking receipt of the product and using it

The problem with this is that when a client calls to place an order or book a coaching session, they are in 'buying mode'. It sounds good, but it isn't. They have already diagnosed their own problem, found the solution and now they are just looking for a supplier who can deliver it quickly at the lowest price. When a client is in buying mode, there is hardly any room for you to differentiate your service and you can only compete on speed and price.

Asking questions means that you can understand how the client arrived at their decision, and you can understand the information that was available to them.

As for the image of a salesperson as someone who likes to tell the client how much he or she knows about the product, the market or what is best for the client, here's another old saying...

> ## The client doesn't care how much you know until they know how much you care

Listening to the client, understanding their needs and making sure that you know as much background as possible will ensure that what you deliver isn't just what the client asked for, it's much more than that.

Ultimately, delivering what the client asked for is the most basic service that you can provide. The client will be satisfied, but probably won't think twice about it.

Understanding the client, anticipating their needs and helping them to solve their problems is what will delight a client and give them a reason to recommend you to others, or to act as a reference for case studies.

8.2 Decisions

The sales cycle is a sequence of decisions. We need to understand what happens during each of these, and what that means for the role of the salesperson.

In order for you to make a decision about anything, you need these three things:

- Information

- Outcome

- Need

So that's like a decisION then.

Think about something you've bought. You needed Information, about what was available, you had a Need to solve a problem and you had an Outcome in mind, so you imagined what would solve your problem.

Sometimes your problem is more tangible, such as running out of milk or facing a huge repair bill for your car, and sometimes your problem is more conceptual, such as the problem created by advertising which makes you think you need something only because you don't already have it.

Earlier, I talked about the balance of risk, and actually this takes place at every decision point.

You buy milk on the way home because you have run out of milk (Need) and you want to have a nice cup of tea this evening (Outcome). You pass a shop (Information) so you stop to buy milk. At this point you are balancing the risk of the milk not meeting your expectations with the cost, so you check the 'best before' date before paying for the milk, because the most likely risk is that the milk will be off, or is 'short dated' so that it will be off before you finish using it. The risk will be that you think you can have milk on your cereal, but you can't because it's gone off.

If your lifestyle means that milk frequently goes off before you've finished using it, you might mitigate the risk by buying long life milk and keeping a stock in your kitchen cupboard.

Every decision you make edges you closer to a purchase. Do you want milk? Do you have milk? Do you have time to buy milk? Will you pass a shop on the way home that sells milk? Will the shop have milk in stock? Will the milk be within its 'best before' date? Will you have enough money?

You're not aware of this sequence of decisions, yet they influence your behaviour. With a bigger purchase such as a car or house, or your decision to change jobs, you're much more aware of the decision points and the risks that have to balance out at each decision point in order for you to move forwards.

This reveals an absolutely critical point about sales in general – that at any point in the decision process, your objective is **not** to sell, it is only to move the client to the next decision point.

No matter how hard I try to sell you milk, or a new car, or a house, if you don't currently need one, you won't buy it. That doesn't mean that you'll never buy those things from me, it just means that you won't buy them *now*.

Sales 'experts' and trainers generally simplify this, saying that the client or prospect doesn't have a need. That's not true. You do have a need for milk, a car and a house, but if those needs are currently met then you won't make a decision to move on in the buying process. However, you might make a decision, right now, to make a note of the new convenience store that's opened around the corner, or the car you saw yesterday that you like the look of, or the new housing development by the river that might be worth a look in the future.

Sales targets make salespeople artificially focus on what they can win before their next bonus, but this usually comes at the expense of developing a pipeline of future business.

When you think in terms of moving your prospects to the next decision point, you're no longer focusing only on the prospects who are ready to place an order.

I'm sure you have a friend who you only hear from when they want something. You might also know someone who is only nice to you when they want something. How do you feel about them? That's how we feel about salespeople who only call when we've got money to spend.

When you're supporting your prospect through the series of decision points, you're only focusing on moving to the next decision point. So when you're just starting to think about a new car, a salesperson rambling on about financing or their fantastic extended warranty is irrelevant, and will quite likely put you off, because you're not at the point where you can consider such things.

I'm sure you've experienced such a pushy 'hard sell', and it feels pushy because the salesperson is trying to jump ahead of where you are in your decision process. No matter how much I ask a bag of flour if it's ready to place an order yet, it still takes 2 hours for my breadmaker to produce bread. There's just no way to take a short cut.

There are ways that some salespeople and retailers try to push the prospect ahead of their decision process. They might include anything from time-limited discount offers to outright threats, such as, "Today is the last day of this opportunity, if you think about it overnight then tomorrow will be too late, you have to go ahead now!" Yeah, right, I'm sure you will still be happy to take my money tomorrow.

While we've seen the concept of the 'sales cycle' to show the general stages that the sales process will progress through, in fact what we really have is a much more intricate series of decisions which either lead to a purchase or not. At every stage, the ultimate decision is to continue or not, and that's a decision as much for you as it is for your prospect. After all, you don't have to do business with everyone you meet, and they don't have to do business with you.

Any sales process moves forwards as a series of tiny steps, no bigger than the risk that either the client or the supplier is willing to take. The equation that makes the trade equal will always balance out at any point in the sales cycle.

During the first contact, the client is unlikely to commit to the full scope of services, although that depends on how big their problem is. Similarly, at the end of the sales cycle, the supplier trusts the client enough to deliver the services before payment has been made.

This is very important to remember at the beginning of the sales cycle when you're prospecting. When most people think about making sales calls, also known as cold calls, they get very nervous. This is because they think that the objective of making such calls is to sell. This is absolutely not true.

The objective at every step of the sales cycle is only to move to the next step, or to qualify out. In order to do that, you need more information, so always your objective throughout the whole sales cycle is to gather more information. This enables both you and your prospect to balance the risk.

This is less of a problem with product sales, where the customer can try out the product and return it if they don't like it. Many retailers have adopted a 'no questions asked' returns policy in order to reduce the risk of getting the customer to make a decision. This is very important in online retail where the customer can very easily shop around with absolutely nothing to encourage loyalty. At least if you're talking to the customer face to face, they will associate you with good service and might feel bad about going somewhere else just for a slightly better price. Such price comparisons are only possible where two products are identical, so retailers often bundle accessories to make it impossible for the customer to make direct comparisons.

In service sales, the issue of balancing risk is much more complex and difficult to overcome. Again, we have the issue of the client comparing service based on an expected outcome.

Let's say that you offer a mobile oven cleaning service, so the outcome is a clean oven. Every oven cleaning service has the same outcome, so the customer can't tell one from another. Typically, the customer's decision criteria will move to cost and time, so how much is the service, and can you come out today.

In order to differentiate, you might offer a free consultation, maybe a bundle of oven care products, a guarantee, a half price second visit and so on. What you're trying to do is make it seem that the customer gets much more for their money with you, whilst at the same time minimising your additional costs.

The higher the perceived value, the bigger the risk the customer will take, up until the point at which it seems too good to be true.

The problem with such differentiators is that you have to put them in your advertising for them to make a difference, at which point they're very easy for your competitors to copy. Statements such as "as seen on TV" or "New York's number one home repair service" are harder to copy, because they have to be true. Advertising statements are covered by the Sale of Goods and Services Act. However, you'll find that your local media and chamber of commerce do run ranking and recommendation services, and if you have something newsworthy, it's not that difficult to get on local radio or even television.

All of these differentiators serve the same purpose, to increase the perceived value of your services so that the customer feels that they're taking a smaller risk. When the customer feels that the risks balance out, they will take a step forwards.

I said that the objective at every step of the sales cycle is only to move to the next step, or to qualify out. The purpose of the first phone call is to agree a meeting. The purpose of the meeting is to gather information. The purpose of gathering information is to produce a price, and so on. When the customer has a clear idea of what your service will provide at what price, and has a clear understanding of how your service meets their needs, they will take the step forward which involves signing a contract for you to go ahead. However, even that isn't the end of the process.

A good indication of the prospect's perception of risk is their willingness to give information. You might want to know about the size of their business, current suppliers, current problems and so on. However, the prospect knows that they are being sold to, and they will be naturally resistant to that, and they won't want to give you information which might give you an advantage over them.

A common example is home energy providers. They will start by making a proposition – to save money on your energy bills. Their underlying belief is that everyone wants to save money. When you acknowledge that you would like to save money, they move to the next step and ask you what you're currently paying and who your current supplier is, so that they can calculate just how much you'll save. At this point, they can't guarantee saving you anything, but again their belief is that they will, hence they say that they'll calculate how much you'll save, not if you'll save anything or not.

You're now faced with a decision, You either have to give the salesperson some information, or risk losing out. Most people, focused on the idea of saving money, will give the information, rationalising 'what harm can it do?'. The information itself doesn't really give the supplier any advantage, the much more important fact that is that you have made a concession and given the supplier something that they have asked for. You have also invested time in the relationship, and you are now less likely to invest the same time with one of their competitors.

When you're selling your services, you can move the sales process along more quickly by asking your prospects for information. It doesn't really matter what information you ask for, because what you're doing is getting them to make concessions, which will accelerate the sales process as it develops.

The fundamental question that every prospect will ask before they can feel comfortable to go ahead is, "Do I trust this person to do what they say they will do?"

9: Sales Data

Good sales people are organised, methodical and their decisions about what to do are driven by sales data. Most of all, they know that their most valuable asset is their own time.

In turn, sales data is part of the information required to run a business. Understanding sales data is critical in managing a business, because sales data represents all of the income that a business earns in order to pay its employees and suppliers. A business exists to sell products and services, and the reality of life is that clients don't turn up on your doorstep with their cheque books in their hands; you have to go and find them. It's therefore very important to know which activities lead to sales so that you can focus your efforts for maximum returns.

You'll also need to know when to expect that income. An employee knows when it's pay-day and plans accordingly for important purchases such as takeaway pizza and beer. Thus, the last Friday of the month is generally the busiest in the pubs and bars of your local town centre.

By understanding how much it costs to make a profit, you know how to work out the minimum that you can sell a product or service for.

How to Sell Coaching

Profit = Sales revenue − Fixed costs − Variable costs

What your customers pay

Rent
Council tax
Employed staff
Depreciation
Internet

Cost of sale
Raw materials
Waste
Contract staff
Electricity
Telephone
Transport

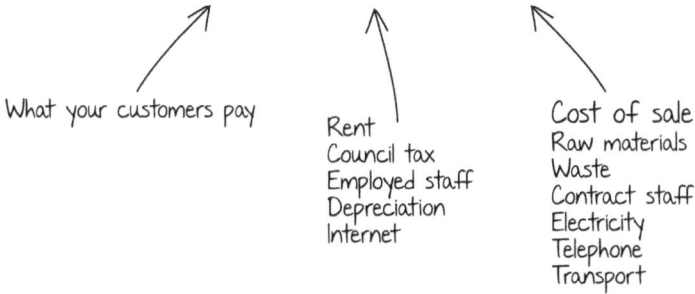

Costs for different things work differently though.

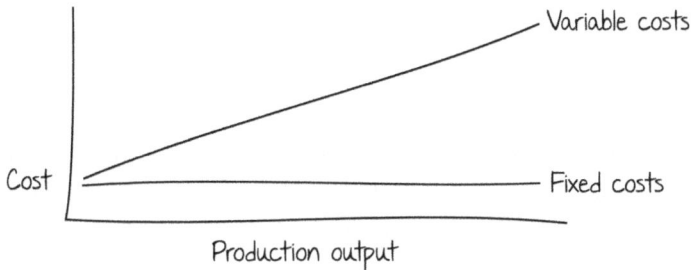

Variable costs

Cost

Fixed costs

Production output

There are some 'fixed costs' which don't change with usage or demand, so we have to make sure that our total sales income will be high enough to cover those to begin with. Therefore, we have to be confident that we're going to sell enough to cover those fixed costs. Then we have 'variable costs'. These increase as we sell or produce more, so we have to make sure that our sales margin on each sale covers those costs.

I often see business owners hiring sales people and telling them to sell as much as they can, because lots of sales is good. Lots of sales is not good. Predictable sales is good so that you can plan for pay day.

One of the most important measurements in sales is your **conversion ratio**.

At each stage of the process, you will reduce the number of clients that you are dealing with. You could say that each stage of the sales cycle serves to focus your time and effort onto the people most likely to buy from you. You'll achieve this by 'qualifying' each prospect, and by asking more questions at the qualification stage, your sales process will become more efficient.

If you send out 1,000 prospecting emails and receive 10 replies then your conversion rate at that stage is 1%. By identifying the points in your sales cycle at which potential clients make decisions, and by calculating the conversion ratios at each point, you can target your time and effort, thereby increasing your conversion rates. Because higher conversion rates lead to either more orders or fewer prospects, your cost of sale reduces and your profits increase.

Sales people often talk about a 'pipeline' or 'funnel':

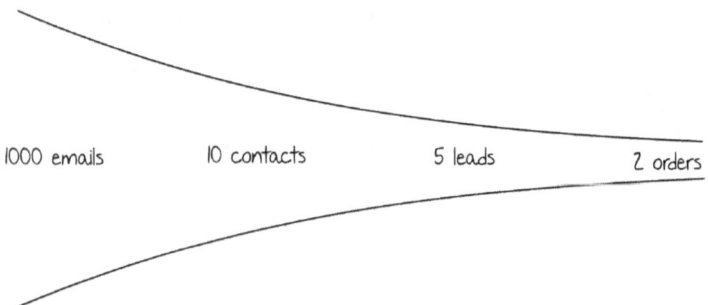

1000 emails   10 contacts   5 leads   2 orders

When you know your conversion ratios, you can calculate how many prospects will generate the income needed for the business, and you can target your lead generation to attract the types of people who are more likely to buy from you.

You will also know, from experience, the length of time it takes for a prospect to enter this 'pipeline' and then pop out the other end as a client. You'll know this because you've understood the sequence of decisions taken by your prospects and the time that it takes them to progress through those decisions. You'll know, for example, how long it takes your clients to use a pint of milk or update their car.

Let's say that for every 100 enquiries you receive, you win 10 orders, and that the average order value is £500. The total order value is £5,000, but to earn that £5,000, you have to deal with 90 enquiries which don't result in orders. If you focus on the £5,000 that you brought in, you'll overlook the value of the time that you lost to those 90 enquiries. The more time you spent talking to those 90 people, the higher your cost of sale.

If the business requires an income of £3,000,000 per year, that means you have to bring in 6,000 orders per year, which is 500 orders per month, roughly 25 per working day. To win 25 orders a day, you have to deal with 250 enquiries. To do that, you need a big enough sales team, which increases your fixed and variable costs to the point where your profits decline.

Phew. It's not as easy as it looks. Certainly it's not as easy as just selling as much as you can.

A common problem for inexperienced sales people is that they regard everyone they're talking to as a client. Up until the point that money changes hands, the person you're talking to is a prospect, not a client. If you think of people you're just talking to as clients, you'll think that every conversation is valuable, when in fact most of the conversations that you'll have will be a complete waste of your precious, limited and valuable time.

When you have worked out how much money you need to earn each month to cover your living costs, your business costs and your bonus, you then have to work out, from your conversion rate and average order value, just what that means in terms of sales activity.

9.1.1   Your conversion plan

Your turnover or sales target:

Your average order value:

How many orders you need, per:

Year

Month

Week

Day

Knowing your conversion ratios means that you know exactly what to focus on now to deliver the right income for the business tomorrow.

You also need to understand the typical lead time for taking a prospect through the sales cycle. Do you get a phone call one day, book the client in the next and get paid by the end of the week? Or do you need to talk to a prospect multiple times, send them information to think about, chase them up, fit around their holidays and then wait 30 days for payment?

A very common mistake that sales people make is that that when the bank balance is looking a little worse for wear, they immediately start trying to close every enquiry that's on their 'to do' list. You'll see such people quite often, posting on social media. Their desperation is obvious, and it's not attractive for potential clients.

If you want payments today then you needed to be working with clients a week or a month ago, and you needed to be talking to them two months ago, and you needed to be writing articles and posting on social media three months ago.

Your focus should never be on chasing clients who might place an order, it should be on engaging with new prospects and then staying engaged with those prospects as they move along their decision process.

The time it takes a prospect to shuffle through your sales cycle is called the average sales cycle time, which is the time from the first point of contact with a prospect to the receipt of their order. In some businesses, this can be as long as 6 to 12 months, perhaps even longer, so if your income is falling, there's little that you can do that will impact it in the short term.

When income declines, every sales manager I've ever met wants the sales team to focus on the 'low hanging fruit', as in, the deals which are due to close shortly, or which can be closed shortly with a bit of pressure. You now know that the deals which are due to close shortly will close anyway, one way or the other, therefore the logical course of action is to sit tight and increase prospecting activities. No-one does that, though. What most corporate sales people will do is offer the prospect an incentive to place and order early, usually in the form of a discount. Poor planning has directly reduced profits!

Knowing your conversion rates means that you can manage your activity now to deliver the right revenue in the future. It's the same in manufacturing; if something goes wrong at the start of the process, it's too late to do a quality check only at the end. You have to check quality at every stage of the production process, and in sales, we need to check quality, or conversions, at every stage too.

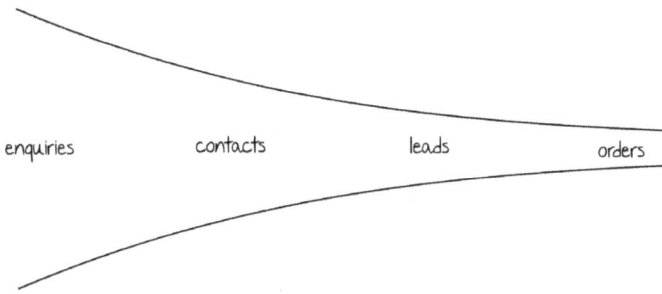

| enquiries | contacts | leads | orders |

Just selling more is not a good way to increase profits. Because British Leyland miscalculated the production cost of the Mini in the 1970s, they made a small loss on each car sold. The Mini was very successful, so those small losses turned into big losses.

Once you know your decision points and conversion ratios, you know exactly what you need to do today to bring in orders tomorrow, next month and next year.

Good sales people spread the risk of the projects they are working on, so that they have a balance of short, medium and long sales cycles. Long sales cycles tend to mean that you're talking to the prospect before they are ready to buy, however that is useful because it 'locks out' your competitors and enables you to influence the buyer's decision. It's not going to pay the bills today, though, hence a balance is needed.

9.1.2 Conversion ratios

List the decision points in your sales cycle, a point at which you have some form of contact with a prospect, at which that prospect makes a decision to move to the next stage or not.

Then work out your conversion ratio at each point, and based on how many people you are actively engaging with.

Decision Point:

Qty per Day/ Week/ Month:

Conversion Ratio:

9.1.3 Order value

When you know your average order value, you can calculate how many prospects you need to be engaging with each day to generate the level of income that you need.

Target revenue:

Average order value:

Prospects per Day/Week/Month:

I was asked to deliver some sales coaching for a company that sold services to the health and fitness industry. They had one salesperson who only had to answer the phone because their events and online marketing generated incoming sales leads.

The owner of the business told me that they used to have a saleswoman who was fantastic, always on the phone, laughing and chatting with callers and, critically, winning lots of orders. She left, and the new guy just wasn't living up to their expectations. The owner's inclination was to fire him, but thought it only fair to give him some support first.

The salesman was making some obvious mistakes, but nothing really serious. For example, if a caller didn't decide to go ahead, he'd then ask for their contact details so that he could follow up. Of course, they made their excuses and said they'd call him, and he never heard from most of them again.

I got him to take their details as soon as they called on the pretence of being able to call them if they got cut off. At this point, the caller hasn't received the information they want, so they are more willing to trade their contact details in order to meet their particular needs.

This meant that he could then follow up, and of the people who he followed up with, some said no and some said, "I was just talking to my friend about you last night. You know, if I carry on procrastinating I'm never going to do this. Go on then, I'll go ahead." so his overall conversion rate improved.

This brings us to the fundamental problem in this story – the business owners only knew that they had a sales problem when they checked their bank balance. They had no idea how enquiries turned into money in the bank. By putting in place some very simple metrics and using those to tweak the salesman's behaviour, his performance steadily improved. After two weeks, we discovered something very interesting – he was outselling the 'fantastic' saleswoman by a considerable margin. He was by far a better salesperson than she had been. What this revealed was something the owners didn't know – the number of incoming leads had halved over the previous year. The new guy was getting close to her sales order value with half the number of leads. The owners realised they had to change their marketing in order to increase the number of leads. A specific issue that this highlighted was the activity of a new competitor who were taking market share from my client – again, something the owners hadn't noticed.

Their instinct, to look at the sales guy, wasn't necessarily misplaced, but their belief in his failure was. When I started working with him, his performance was just average. At the end of the four coaching sessions, his performance was outstanding. Yes, of course that was thanks to my brilliant coaching and considerable sales expertise. Alternatively, it was thanks to some simple metrics which showed us where the gaps were and what to do about them. The salesperson was just an average guy, which means that he was smart and efficient, a fast learner and able to focus on results.

Remember, you can't improve what you don't measure, simply because you won't know whether you've improved it or not.

10:   Prospecting

Prospecting is all of the various activities you might undertake when looking for potential clients.

Prospecting activities can include:

- Cold calling

- Networking

- Social media

- Direct mail

- Advertising

- Joining business networks

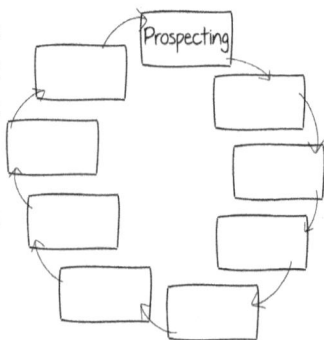

Each of these has a different cost, a different time requirement and a different rate of return. However, you can expect them all to have roughly the same cost of sale. If you find a prospecting method that gives you a significantly lower cost of sales then make the most of it while you can!

Targeted online advertising, for example, costs more on a pay-per-click basis than non-targeted advertising because you have to do less of it to reach the same number of qualified prospects.

Just because a prospecting method doesn't cost much doesn't make it cheap because the potentially lower conversion rate will make the cost of acquiring a new client about the same.

10.1.1 Cost of sale

What are the components of your cost of sale?

When you add up these direct and indirect costs, you can see how much it costs you to earn every Pound/Dollar/Rupee/Yen of income from sales.

A telemarketing agency that I knew ran a direct marketing campaign, making 2500 calls for a client with the objective of securing sales meetings.

After making 2500 'cold calls', the agency secured 14 appointments. This is a conversion rate of 0.56% which is not bad for cold calling.

In 2010, it took 4 calls to reach a decision maker. In 2012, it took 41 calls. We are all increasingly exposed to sales messages, and we become naturally more resistant over time.

I'm not going to talk about specific cold calling techniques here, there are many books on that subject alone which you can read if that's a prospecting activity that you want to pursue. In this book, I want to convey an overall systematic approach to selling rather than focusing on techniques. What I will say is that cold calling doesn't work, or it does work, depending on whether it fits with your overall business model. What absolutely does not work is making ten cold calls, feeling disheartened and declaring cold calling to be a failure. With a 0.56% success rate, you can see that you need to make 179 calls to guarantee getting a meeting. That is a lot of calls. Let's say that the average call time is a minute, that's still three hours.

Cold calling is probably better suited to product sales than for service, because a product is easier for the prospect to understand and identify a need for. I know right away if I need new ink cartridges for my printer or new home improvement products. However, if you're offering car servicing or business consultancy then the chance of me needing that right now are slim. In fact, the chance of me needing home improvement products is slim, which is why those companies have a bad reputation for their sales approach.

With a service, it's much harder for the prospect to get a good impression quickly through cold calling. Not impossible though, and because you'll be adopting a systematic approach to what you do, you'll try different angles and messages and measure what works best, rather than just using the trite and clichéd sales pitches out of a book. A different book, obviously.

Most importantly, remember that the best sales people don't prospect on Friday afternoons, or only when the bank balance is looking a little worse for wear. They are prospecting always, every day. Every time you post on social media, you're prospecting - if that's your focus, and you share your message consistently.

10.2   Cold Calling

Sooner or later, any salesperson has to pick up the telephone and call a potential client. Many people call this 'cold calling' and this can make the process unnecessarily difficult for many sales people. It hardly sounds inviting, does it?

Whether you make sales calls from a list or to follow up on warm contacts from an introduction or networking event, at some point you do have to pick up the phone.

Some sales people excel at making sales calls, however many find it very hard. Whilst many sales people find it difficult to get into a routine with their sales calls, there is often a process that we can uncover.

For example, if you get variable results when making sales calls, you may have the right skills but an inconsistent process. If you get consistent but undesirable results, the process is working perfectly and it's the content you need to change.

Easily making sales calls is such an important aspect of the sales person's job that I'm going to share with you an article I wrote for a magazine on exactly this subject:

Making prospecting calls is one of the most important, and most feared parts of a sales person's job. The other day, I received this email from a sales person I worked with recently:

"I would just like to say a BIG, BIG thanks, I feel totally transformed, my 'phone fear' has disappeared. Its really quite weird, but I don't hesitate to pick the phone and ring people, in the past 10 days I've picked up 4-5 briefs. When I see an opportunity I just grab it.

I've noticed a big difference in my day too, I just don't know where the hours go, and I wish there were longer hours in the day to fit everything in. This will make you laugh, the last few days I've had lots of admin work, and haven't been able to get on the phone, I actually heard myself saying that 'I wish I was on the phone more' can you believe it?"

What would it be like if you felt the same way about your sales calls? Now, in order for you to be succeeding at your job, you must already be making sales calls, so I'm not talking about teaching you the basics here. I'm presuming you already do make calls, but maybe you tidy your desk, answer your emails and make a cup of coffee before you get yourself into the right mood. Maybe you stop after ten calls instead of stopping when the clients have all gone home. Maybe you make it harder for yourself than it needs to be.

Maybe you already love sales calls and you're already getting great results, in which case – why are you reading this? Get on the phone!

A change like this can happen very quickly. The longest this has ever taken was about an hour, the shortest about one minute.

But how? Well, the exact process varies from one person to the next because every person I've ever worked with creates this situation in a slightly different, unique way – and so will you. Having said that, there are some general principles and patterns that I can tell you about that you can use right away to improve your approach and therefore your results.

Firstly, stop cold calling. It's difficult, time consuming and produces poor results. Instead, spend some time each day calling people you haven't spoken to before and finding out how you can help them.

Secondly, At the moment you pick up the phone to dial, what picture pops into your head? What does the voice in your head say? Do you begin your call by apologising, or does your voice tone demonstrate the pride you take in your job? Just work through these simple steps, giving yourself time to think this through very carefully:

Imagine yourself sitting at your desk at the time you would begin making sales calls. As you imagine starting to dial, what picture pops into your head. Specifically, whose picture? If you find sales calls consistently difficult, I'm guessing the picture is of someone you don't have much in common with who doesn't look pleased to hear from you. If you find calls randomly difficult, I'm guessing there's no coherent picture. In either case, that's good news.

Next, imagine you're about to call your best friend or someone you like very, very much. You know exactly what I mean. As you dial, what picture pops into your mind? Now, stop and think about yourself – are you smiling? Are you sitting upright? Are you dialling eagerly? When you speak, does your tone of voice reflect this?

So, if you imagine someone who doesn't want to talk to you, simply imagine reaching out and grabbing the picture, screwing it into a ball and throwing it over your shoulder. Then simply draw a new picture of someone who looks like you, who you have something in common with and who looks pleased to hear from you, or at least open minded. Imagine calling that person and notice how your voice tone is different.

Practice this a few times, repeating the process over and over. Imagine starting to dial, see the face of someone you want to talk to, hear your positive voice tone, notice how that feels nice to talk to someone who enjoys talking to you.

Thirdly, what do you say to yourself before, during and after the call? If it's in any way critical that's not helping. Often, the voice in your head has really valuable feedback but you don't hear it because it just sounds like nagging or criticism. Think again about sitting down to make your calls and this time pay attention to what you are saying to yourself. Change the voice tone to something more neutral, like a news reader, or to a voice that you like – even something sexy! Now, listen to what the voice tells you – is the information more useful? You can also ask questions back. If the voice is critical, say, "Thank you! Now, how does that information help me?" or, "Thank you! Now, what do you suggest I do differently?" Oddly enough, you'll find the same approach works very well with that person in the office who always offers you helpful criticism.

Last of all, you can't really control what happens during each call as you are not in control of the person at the other end. They might be busy or tired and you know the importance of respecting their state. So, no matter how each call goes, it's important to treat each call as if it's your first. There are many ways that you can quickly control your state, and the simplest for our purposes here is through your focus of attention. Think of a time in the past when you felt really confident and in control of yourself. Remember that time in all the detail you can, recalling what you saw, heard and felt. Maybe you even remember some smells and tastes. When you have all that, think of a word, colour or piece of music that seems to represent it.

Repeat this a few times so that the trigger becomes associated with the feeling. Now, in between calls simply replay the trigger and your state will switch to the confident, in control state.

After you have practised all this for a day and then slept on it, your brain will build it into an unconscious calling routine for you so you won't even have to think in order to get good results. What's this based on? The principle that you are already following an unconscious process which is working perfectly for you. The process is fine but the results need a little tweak. By taking conscious control over the process and making some slight adjustments, you'll find that you can get surprising results, very quickly. How quickly? You'll only find out by finding out!

10.3   Social Media

Social media websites are valuable prospecting tools. LinkedIn is currently the best tool to use, but you should also make the most of the social features of sites more relevant to your clients. I know a coach who generates enquiries through Instagram, so anything is possible if you focus and deliver a consistent message.

When you make contact with a new client, you can invite them to LinkedIn or to like your Facebook page. Use it to keep track of what they're doing, who they're talking to and to send them regular updates about developments or events that might interest them.

You can also use LinkedIn to find new prospects by searching within companies or industries, or looking through the connections of your colleagues and even your competitors. LinkedIn will, from time to time, offer you free trials of their premium service. Take advantage of these and use them to search for new clients. Whilst this may be better suited to an indirect sales approach than for finding direct clients, you will get enquiries if you have a consistent message.

If you're active on LinkedIn then you have probably been approached by 'sales experts' who promise to skyrocket your coaching business and bring you a constant flow of new sales leads. I receive at least one a day, here are two screenshots from my LinkedIn messages on two consecutive days.

Hi Peter

If you're using LinkedIn, but still not seeing a return on investment of your pressure time - this may just be what you are looking for?

We are a lead-generating service and we guarantee results every month.

We Connect with Customers with:

A proven system to deliver sales leads on demand.
Consistent leads - never rely on "hit-or-miss" marketing campaigns.
Convert leads into appointments
You have complete control, turn the flow of leads "on or off" whenever you want.

> Hi Peter
>
> It is great to be connected in these exciting and yet "crazy" times.
> There's a new energy in the market place and I see many people looking at new ways of doing things.
>
> I'm reaching out to you because I help business owners - consultants and advisors generate 2-5 HIGH VALUE leads per day on LinkedIN.
>
> Working with people all over the world, helping them to get a deeper understanding of their ideal client and building stronger connections that turn into HIGH TICKET customers. Which means that you can become more effective and successful with LESS EFFORT and have more free time to focus on what you truly love!

Is it a good idea to use such services? No.

Why not? Because this is marketing, not sales, and marketing is safe. The results are unverifiable. They use their click funnels to grab email addresses and call those leads. Leads are not money in the bank. If you don't understand the sales process then you don't understand why leads are almost worthless.

An email address is not a lead. A lead is the full contact details for a named person who has explicitly expressed an interest in you and your services.

These marketing experts are of course preying on your fear of selling. They promise to do all of the hard work for you, but there are two lies hidden in their promises.

Firstly, they are offering leads, not clients. A lead is the start of the sales process, you still have to do all of the hard work. If you can 'turn the flow of leads on or off' then that must mean they are producing generic leads for any coach, not specifically for you.

Secondly, getting leads is easy if you're forcing people to trade an email address for a free ebook or personality profile or other information product. You could do that yourself.

Overall, there are two major downsides to using social media for marketing; firstly, everyone else is doing it, and secondly, the social media site owns the prospects, not you. For this reason, many credible marketing experts advocate building your own email list.

10.4   Email

You might associate email marketing with 'spam', and if the email is only trying to get you to buy something, and especially if it is unsolicited then this is certainly fair. Marketing emails in the UK and EU fall under the legislation of the General Data Protection Regulations (GDPR).

The simplest and safest way to build an email list is to use a ready-made service such as Mailchimp. Its free service is generous and they take care of list management and data protection, so you don't have to worry about it. There are others of course, but if you want to see what the user experience is like for Mailchimp, join my newsletter at www.nenlp.com - do you see what I did there? Seriously, though, it's very good. Informative, thought provoking, educational and with only the minimum of advertising for my products and services. Just as a newsletter should be. This style of marketing is often called 'content marketing' because prospects are given valuable content in anticipation of them coming back to buy from you in the future. Of course, most of the people who see your content will consume it and never pay you a penny/dime/rupee/bhat, but that's equally true of all marketing. In content marketing, you're not sending out empty drivel pretending to be useful, you're sending out good, high quality, genuinely useful stuff. You're just not sharing everything in one newsletter.

We know that you can learn almost anything for free online. We know that you can pay a lot of money for online courses which are no better than free YouTube videos. It's almost impossible to protect your content any more, despite copyright laws. You can find pirated copies of most of my books if you look hard enough. So what? Most people who download pirate copies of my books were never going to buy them anyway, and maybe a few are so impressed that they then buy the real thing. Who knows? If you can't protect your content, assuming that you think that anything you do is original anyway, then you might as well create value, credibility and a loyal following by sharing it.

With an email list, you own your contacts, they aren't hidden from you by a social media platform. To keep those contacts on your list, just treat them as you would want to be treated.

One of the best content marketing commentators I've seen is Joe Pulizzi. You can join his list and read past newsletters and articles at www.joepulizzi.com

10.5   Networking Events

Local networking events are as popular as ever, with everyone from professional bodies and universities to local law firms and business clubs getting together on a regular basis. I've found that many of these events are attended by small business owners, hoping to find clients, which is not the right approach to take.

For a start, you need to only attend events which are very relevant to you and your business. That's obvious, but it reveals an interesting point about these events – that many people who attend them do so, not to extend their networks, but because they're lonely. When you're lonely, any event will do, and if you find like minded people gripe about how bad things are, you'll find the experience reassuring, if not productive.

Your purpose for attending such an event is not to complain, and it's certainly not to sell because the chances of finding your ideal client at the moment they're ready to buy is highly unlikely. Not impossible, just highly unlikely. Some events are free to attend, some charge. The ones where you're most likely to find a potential client charge the most, of course!

> **You're there to network, not sell**

Whether in person or online, networking events are a valuable and important source of leads.

How do you currently network? Do you network purposefully, visiting conferences, networking events and business groups, or is it an informal process where you just bump into interesting people?

What can you do to network more purposefully, as a way of generating more prospects?

I have met people at networking events who believed that networking doesn't really work and that they might meet one or two people at an event. I go with the intention of getting a business card from everyone there. Now you might say that it's better to have only one or two really good meetings than spend only a couple of minutes with everyone, but here's the problem. When you walk in to a room full of strangers, how do you know who will be the most useful ones to talk to? Potential contacts are everywhere, not just at networking events. I could even say that the people who are really worth knowing don't go to those events, but that really depends on how they're organised and who their target market is.

I have found that people who say you should have only one or two good conversations are usually rationalising their fear of strangers. The people who aim to get round the whole room end up meeting more people, and that is exactly what networking meetings are for. They are not for holding business meetings or doing sales pitches, they are for making contact. It's up to you to follow up on those contacts later on, remembering that the purpose of networking is not to meet customers – it is to grow your network. Converting those connections into clients comes later.

When networking, it's very important that you can tell other people what you do as clearly and concisely as possible. A model called 'logical levels' is a handy way to structure your introduction.

You can start at the Identity level and work down, constructing a short phrase that is easy to remember and flows well. For example, "I'm a leading business coach who helps large and small organisations, teams and individuals get better results, more consistently.

Identity - Who you are

Belief - What's good about that

Capability - What you can do, your skills

Behaviour - What you actually do

Environment - Where or with whom you do it

There are lots of other formats that you can use, the important point is that your introduction flows neatly and is easy to listen to without any logical jumps.

Social networking

If you haven't already figured it out, then you might bear in mind that everything that I'm going to tell you about the best networkers applies as equally to online networking through social media as it does to live events. Grow your network, add value. If you only think about what you want from your contacts, your network will wither and die.

Expert networkers

- Value their contact network

- Are looking for routes, not targets

- Know that their value is not in what they can do but in who they know

The more connections a network has, the more valuable it is. That should be obvious, really, however many people think only about what the network can do for them.

But there's an interesting paradox with good networkers; they end up with lots of business cards, but that's not what they aim for. If someone boasts about how many business cards or LinkedIn connections they have, that tells you that their aim is quantity over quality. They judge their success by their own popularity, but people at networking events often aren't choosy about who they give cards to. It's very easy to go to an event with a hundred people and swap business cards with every single one, but so what?

What are you going to do with those cards? Frame them and hang them on your wall?

Good networkers go to an event with the intention of meeting lots of people, but that is not an end in itself. Their primary goal is to meet as many as possible of the *right* people, and the only way to meet lots of the right people is to meet lots of people, and to then be very selective about who you follow up with, and how.

Good networkers rarely discount a connection as worthless because they have the utmost respect for the people they meet. Instead, they apply a kind of informal grading system based not on someone's air of authority or their important sounding job title but on their ability and willingness to connect to other people.

Goals

Sometimes you will go to a networking event, and everything just falls into place. The right person is there, with the right opportunity, at the right time. But it's more often the case than you'll get results from networking with nothing more complicated than good old fashioned hard work.

Your goal for attending a networking event should be:

Meet as many people as possible

The key to success is that this goal is under your control, whereas finding someone ready to offer you a job is down to pure chance.

As you meet more and more people at networking events, you'll begin to get an idea of the landscape within which you're operating, the players, the people who it's good to know. You'll also meet some hangers-on, people who just like collecting business cards but never quite get round to putting you in touch with the person you want to speak to. They see their network as an asset, only to be used when they want something from someone.

A network is like a garden; to get the most out of it, you occasionally have to do some fairly aggressive pruning.

For now, let's focus on the aspect of networking which puts most people off and enables you to get a real head start on your competitors – going up and talking to strangers.

Introducing yourself

At a party, do you go round introducing yourself to people you don't know? Do you wait to be approached? Or do you head for people you already know and stick to them for the rest of the evening?

People behave in the same way at networking events. If you only speak to people you already know then you might as well have stayed at home. The point of networking is to meet people you don't yet know.

The point of networking is to meet people you don't yet know

According to Dale Carnegie, everyone's favourite subject is themselves, and this is another simple way that you can differentiate yourself. I'm sure you've had conversations where you each seem to be battling to say something interesting about yourself. For many people, the purpose of listening is to be able to say something interesting and relevant. And if they can't make it relevant, change the subject and say it anyway.

Remember your purpose of attending a networking event; it's not to advertise yourself, it's to meet people and find out if they can add value to your network. You can only do that by listening to them, so as quickly as possible you need to turn the conversation round to them, and by far the most important thing to remember when you want to steer a conversation is that you have to have control of it in the first place.

You must make the approach because:

1. You get to choose who to talk to

2. You get to control the conversation

3. You get to find out what you need to know

If you wait to be approached, you're not in control of the conversation. So overcoming any nervousness that you might have about approaching strangers is key to getting results from networking. You also need to understand that it's highly likely that they are more nervous than you are.

There have been many books written about networking, and many networking 'experts' can give you their suggestions for opening lines and contrived sound-bites which sound like adverts for washing powder.

"Hi, I'm John and I can impact on your bottom line through innovation and great team work!"

"Erm... hello John. I was just leaving."

You will no doubt have come across the idea of the 'elevator pitch'. The reason that it's called this is based on a scenario used in sales training, namely that you visit a prospect and happen to get in the elevator, known more properly as a 'lift', with the company's CEO. What do you say to make her or him keen to meet with you and give you all their money? You only have 10 seconds to impress them - what do you say?

The major flaw with the concept of the elevator pitch is that it is designed to be used on someone who is not listening to you, not interested in you, doesn't know you, isn't the decision maker for what you're selling and didn't get in the lift to buy anything. So for our networking purposes, the context is wrong, the format is wrong and the intention is wrong. Apart from that, they're a fabulous idea.

Don't build up networking to be more complicated than it is. All you need to do is meet people, have a short conversation and then move on.

By far the most effective way to start a networking conversation is therefore:

1. Hello, I'm....

2. Who are you?

3. And what are you here for?

This may seem simple, yet it is very carefully structured to make networking as easy and effective as possible. Here's why.

When you make the approach and say hello, you are in control of the conversation. All you need to say is your name, and maybe just your first name to make it easy for the other person to remember.

Once you've introduced yourself, you ask a question. Asking questions is the primary way to maintain control of a conversation, and it also serves the important purpose of finding out who you're talking to!

Let's say that the other person tells you their name and job title. All good information.

Now comes to the really clever part. Instead of getting into a rambling conversation about nothing in particular, you ask a very important question, which is to find out what the other person wants to achieve by attending the event.

By getting them to reveal their purpose, you find out some important information:

□ Are they a good networker?

□ Are they going to be useful for you?

□ Are you going to be useful for them?

And more than that, your question encourages the polite reply, "How about you? What are you here for?"

You can now deliver your master stroke. You see, once people have overcome their fear of approaching strangers, their next problem is that they can't get away. They complain that they spent the whole evening talking to one person and may have missed some good connections. So, in answer to the question, you say, "I'm here to meet new people". In that one sentence, you tell the other person the most important thing of all; that you won't be talking to them all night.

You can now have a short yet meaningful conversation, and when you're ready to move on, simply say, "Well, as I said, I want to meet new people, so I'm going to let you mingle some more too. It's been really good to meet you."

As soon as you walk away, take out your pen and write some notes on the back of the person's card so that you can follow up in a way that is relevant and memorable.

But when do you swap cards? At the end of the conversation, as you say, "we must keep in touch!"

No.

At that point, the other person has already decided whether they want to hear from you again, and they can choose whether to give you a card or say they've run out. No, the time to swap business cards is at the beginning, when you say your name.

> # Swap business cards at the beginning of the conversation, not at the end

Remembering names

One of the things that good networkers do is to remember the names of the people they meet. Some people find this very difficult to do, so I'm going to give you a way of remembering people's names which is absolutely guaranteed to work, every time.

You may have heard that you can recall someone's name by forming a related mental image. If you meet Jack Thomas, you might picture a cartoon cat using a car jack. You have to include the person in the picture to link the face to the name. This all goes pear shaped when you meet Wladislaw Jachtchenko. This method makes good theatre, but is useless in practicality.

The first method, which will greatly increase your retention of the person's name, is to say it out loud. You can easily work this into the conversation, repeating their name as you search for connections. Maybe you know someone with the same surname, or their surname is a place that you can comment on.

The second way, which is guaranteed to work, is to ask for their business card at the start of the conversation. When you look back to check their job title or company you can remind yourself of their name. Later, make a note of something that will help you link the name to the person.

BigCo
Jack Thomas
Boss of Stuff
jthomas@big.co

Big black glasses, red tie
Interested in exec coaching
Email research from ICF
Follow up next week

Breaking the ICE

Often, when you arrive at a networking event, people will have already formed into cliques; small, tightly knit groups that exclude newcomers.

How would you break into a clique?

A senior partner in an accounting practice was a master at working his way into established groups.

A junior partner wanted to learn how to achieve this miracle, so he went to a networking event and stood within earshot so that he could listen in.

What he observed was that the senior partner would approach the edge of a clique, say something, and the clique would magically open up and allow him in.

What do you think the senior partner said? What do you think his magic words were?

> # Hello chaps!

That's all there was to it!

So let's put together everything you've learned about networking so far and break the ICE:

> # Introduce → Chat → Exit

Introduce yourself, remembering to say that you're there to meet lots of people.

Chat, about what you want for as long as you want.

Exit gracefully, reminding the other person that you're helping them to be better networkers too, by giving them the opportunity to meet more people.

A network is like a garden

- You have to plant seeds

- You have to pull out weeds

- You have to cultivate it

- You have to put in before you can take out

- Once planted, it grows all by itself

The worst mistake

Networking is easy. All you have to do is talk to people and get their contact details. If they don't want to share their details, they're not interested in networking. Move on. Following up after the event is where you qualify your new contacts and build your strategy.

There is really only one thing which you must never, never, ever do at a networking event. OK, maybe two things. But the most important is that you must never sell. Back in the old days when coaching was 'taking off', I would see countless coaches at networking events answering the question, "What is coaching?", even if the other person hadn't asked, by giving an impromptu coaching demonstration. Why? Because the coaching schools tell people that the best way to sell coaching is to demonstrate it. I feel that the glazed look in the other person's eyes disproves this. Giving a coaching demo isn't wrong in itself, it's that no-one went to that networking event to look for a demo.

Imagine meeting a civil engineer at a party, asking what that is and then having him dig a trench in your living room to show you. If you can't sell it without giving a demo, it's because you don't know what it is. Save your coaching for when the client is paying you for it.

Follow up

When you get home from a networking event, email every person who gave you a business card:

- How much you enjoyed meeting them

- What you can do for them

- What you'd like them to do for you

And most important of all, keep in touch. After all, how do you feel about someone who you only hear from when they want something?

Your network will grow because you put effort into it. That doesn't mean a regular email asking, "Do you have any jobs?", it means the occasional email saying, "I saw this news story and thought of you", or, "I just saw your new branding on a van, it looks really good!"

The art of networking

Here's the sequence in full:

1. Say hello, introduce yourself, give a business card and ask for one in return

2. Ask, "What are you here for?"

3. Say, "I'm here to meet new people"

4. Have a brief conversation about anything

5. Say, "Well, as I said, I want to meet new people, so I'm going to let you mingle some more too. It's been really good to meet you."

6. Shake hands and walk away

7. Make notes on the back of their card

8. After the event, follow up

10.6   When the Going Gets Tough

The tough get going? Only in Billy Ocean's song.

I think that I may have mentioned elsewhere in this book that when most self employed coaches look in their wallet, purse, handbag, manbag, billfold or sporran and see a big hole where some money should be, their first instinct is to panic and post on social media about their availability for new clients, and to start pushing harder on anyone who they're talking to about coaching.

Most corporate sales people, when faced with an impending target deadline, will focus on trying to convert any prospects, suddenly switching to 'hard sell' tactics, discounts and other incentives.

This is more likely to push away any tentative prospects, only making the situation worse.

As difficult as it seems, when the going gets tough, it's because you have been resting on your laurels instead of building your 'pipeline' of new prospects. When the going gets tough, don't start closing, start prospecting. Yes, there will be a delay until those prospects convert. Learn your lesson, and use this as a reminder.

The mantra of sales shouldn't be 'Always Be Closing'. It should be 'Always Be Prospecting'.

11:   Qualifying

Good sales people value
their time, so they qualify
every sales lead to make sure
it's worth investing in.

Even if you have plenty of
time to deal with every lead,
you still need to qualify them
because otherwise you are
wasting time that you could be spending doing
something more valuable.

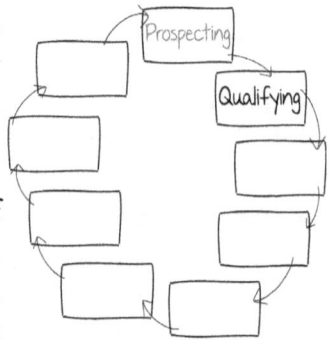

In order to be able to qualify each lead or prospect,
you have to know what you want out of a client. Just
because they have a requirement for your service
doesn't mean that they will definitely buy *your* service.

Once you get into a conversation with a prospect, you
have to identify their problems as soon as possible.
No-one ever hired a plumber or a lawyer just to see
what it's like. They hire service providers to solve
problems.

A prospect will have a conversation with you because
they have a problem to solve. However, for many
personal development services, the catch is that they
won't tell you what that problem is until they trust you,
and they won't trust you until they have told you what
their problem is, and experienced your empathy.

While they will go great lengths to hide their problem, they will tell you what it is in the first minute of your conversation, by telling you that everything is just fine.

Just think about it for a moment. Imagine that you see someone in the street, limping. If you ask them if they need any help, they say, "No thanks, I'm fine". Do you believe them? What are they telling you by limping? They tell you that they are in some pain, that perhaps they have a problem with their leg.

What are they telling you by saying they're fine? They are telling you that they really don't want you to help them. Why would that be?

We might try and guess, but an easy way to figure out the answer is simply to put yourself in their shoes. Imagine that you're in the same situation, why would you deny the offer of help? Maybe you don't want someone to hurry you, making the problem worse. Maybe you don't want to appear vulnerable, for fear of being taken advantage of. What you hide from the world reveals your fears and weaknesses. Strong, fit people tend not to limp.

Therefore, the client will inadvertently tell you what their real problem is, right at the start of the conversation, and with nothing more than empathy and tact, you can easily figure out what that is.

Many sales people talk about their solutions, but it's very important for you to remember that until the client has a problem, you don't have a solution.

Until the client has a problem, you don't have a solution

We can make a difference between wants and needs. I might like the idea of getting a new car, I might even want a new car, but until I need it, I'm unlikely to take action.

The difference is very simple. We want things that we don't have, and if we don't have them, we don't miss them. However, we need things that we depend on, or which we've lost. Needs are much more powerful drivers than wants.

One of things that you'll notice about many advertising campaigns is that they take things which you might want, and position them so that it suddenly seems like a huge problem that you don't have them. Their aim is to turn your want into a need.

For example, if you look at adverts for toothpaste, they'll take a common experience like being sensitive to heat or cold and make it into a problem, so that now you start to worry that there's something wrong with your teeth, and you start to need a special kind of toothpaste, even though you were quite happy with the one you normally buy. And when do you buy toothpaste? When you run out. When you need to replace it. Otherwise, you don't need it.

Mobile phones are a product where the market is designed to make you change your phone every year or two. The whole system, including the handset manufacturers, the carriers and the retailers, is set up to give you an incentive to change your phone when your contract runs out. The reality is that your contract doesn't run out, you can just stay on your plan and keep your phone. But by creating an idea that something is running out, you feel under pressure to take action.

We don't realise that we have problems with out teeth or cars or mobile phones until an advert tells us that we do, and the way that the advert does that is very simple. If you watch these kinds of adverts closely, you'll notice that they take something that is a common experience, and then they describe it as a problem, and then the present the solution. The definition of a common experience as a problem is called reframing, and the way they do it can be very subtle, for example one character talks about a particular experience, and another character reacts in horror. We empathise with the characters, so we feel the sense of horror at not having white teeth or a new car, and then we empathise with the person who has the problem, and we feel bad because someone else is judging us.

Believe it or not, you can achieve this very easily in your own sales conversations. If you believed that your service is so amazing that everyone in the world should be using it, then you would be genuinely surprised if someone didn't already have it.

If someone told you they didn't have electricity at home, or a TV, or a mobile phone, your reaction would probably be, "What? Why not?"

At this stage you're not saying that they have to buy your service from you, but at the very least they should be getting it somewhere. You don't need to convince them or coerce them, you don't need to tell them why it would be good for them, you only have to be surprised that they don't have it. This sows the seeds of a problem, which you will later offer a solution to.

11.1.1 Ideal client

Define your ideal client.

When you know your ideal client, you can qualify every lead with a set of questions and make an informed decision about how to deal with that lead, how much time to invest, when to invest that time and so on.

11.2 Identifying Your Ideal Client

If you want to work in a particular niche then you might think that it could be difficult to identify clients that meet your narrow criteria. In fact, it's super easy, barely an inconvenience.

I've heard that doctors often experience a common problem, namely that if they go to a party or social event, as soon as they tell someone that they are a doctor, that person immediately tells them about their health problems and in some cases even shows them an embarrassing rash for an on-the-spot diagnosis.

Aside from the fact that they're off duty, it's just not right, is it?

Similarly, plumbers are immediately shown every leaking pipe in the house. Maybe that's not so bad, as they could offer to return at another time, for a fee.

Are you starting to see how easy it is to identify your target clients? You don't have to! People are compelled to tell you about their problems. If you say, "I'm a coach", then you might get some half-interested questions about what that entails, but you're only going to trigger a buying response if that person just happens to be thinking about finding a coach at that precise moment.

We know that people don't have an idea about life change and then immediately act upon it. We know that people will sit with a problem, cope with it and self medicate for months or even years before some a compelling event pushes them over a threshold. One of the events that can trigger a buying response is the availability of a solution.

Let's say you meet someone at a party. You ask them what they do, they tell you about their job. They then ask you the same question, to which you reply, "I help people to make the big life changes that they've been promising themselves but putting off", to which they will give one of two responses:

"Oh, that's nice… anyway…" or

"Oh! Don't get me started! I/my husband/my wife/my friend has been trying for years to…"

And your follow up?

"Well, if it's important to you, I can help you to achieve that.

All you have to do to identify your target clients is tell them what problem you solve, and if they have that problem, or if they know anyone who does, they will compulsively tell you all about it. Your next step is then to establish if they feel strongly enough about the problem to spend money solving it.

Many people can appear to feel strongly about finding a solution but are unwilling to pay for one. They are not your clients. Allow them to do you the favour of putting your competitors out of business instead.

11.3   Qualification Criteria

In sales, questions that we ask to determine if a prospect is likely to become a client are called qualification criteria. They don't automatically rule a lead in or out, they just give you information on which to make a decision that is right for your business at that time. If enquiries are slow, you might feel tempted to apply the criteria less ruthlessly than when you're over-run with clients. Without qualification criteria, you can't ever prioritise based on what's good for the business, so you'll tend to prioritise based on what you like doing most, or on who is shouting the loudest. When you aren't very busy with paid work, you might tend to qualify less carefully so that you can feel good about being busy. This is the most important time to qualify hard because, remember, time is your most valuable asset.

One thing that I can tell you about qualification is that any sale that you will ever lose, any sale that any salesperson has ever lost, can be identified at the qualification stage. You'll spend months working on a deal, only to find that the prospect has no budget set aside, or not enough budget, or they have an interest but not a specific need, or there's no compelling event and so they end up waiting... and waiting... and waiting.

There will only ever be one reason for you to lose a deal, and that's because someone else had more information than you did, someone else asked the questions that you were afraid to ask.

If the prospect doesn't have a compelling event, or budget, do you ignore them? Not necessarily, but you do prioritise accordingly and, most importantly, you focus only on the next decision point and not on the getting the final order.

I have found over the years that I've worked in and around sales that many inexperienced sales people are afraid to ask qualification questions because they don't want to offend the prospect. I recall many meetings with people who loved to chat and take up time but had absolutely no money to spend. When you focus on time as your most valuable asset, your question will always be, "What else could I be doing right now?"

This doesn't only apply to prospective clients. Once you achieve any commercial success, you'll become the target of other coaches offering to work with you. "Hey, let's work together and create something amazing!" Everyone's your friend when they can see you doing what they can't do - earning money. What are they bringing to the party, as it were? At the very least, tell them to go and buy this book!

We're going to define a custom set of qualification criteria just for you, and they might include:

- Decision Maker - Is the person you're talking to able to make a buying decision?

- Time - How much of your time is it going to take to win the order?

- Budget - Can the client realistically afford your service?

- Ability to Pay - Is the client's business financially stable?

- Need - Does the client have a clear need for your service?

- Solution - Are you able to solve the client's problem?

- Cost of Sale / Margin - Is there enough profit to make it worthwhile?

- Effort – Will you need to invest so much time and resource that you're better off doing something else?

- Competition - Do you know who else the client is talking to?

- Compelling event – Why now?

You could even make your criteria into an acronym or mnemonic if you like. The first one I learned, back in 1992, was NETWORKS:

- Need
- Effort
- Timescale
- Who
- Original
- Reason
- Kompetition (sic)
- Solution

For a team of consultants who had trouble with cold calling, I came up with TEAMWIN, which was a play on their company name:

- Timescale
- Effort
- Authority
- Money
- Who else?
- Interest
- Need

You might have different questions depending on whether you are selling directly or indirectly.

Direct coaching client:

- Why now?

- Are they prepared to do the work?

- Do they have the money set aside?

- Is anyone else influencing them?

- Do they have a clear objective

Indirect coaching client:

- What's the business need?

- Where's the Training Need Analysis?

- Who has the budget?

- Who has the final decision?

- Is the end user 'bought in'?

- What reporting is expected?

- Is this developmental or remedial?

- What are the measures of success?

- What other services do they need?

11.3.1 Define your qualification criteria

Make a list of your own qualification criteria and questions to help you identify the right types of client for you. This will also help you to make your social media posts more targetted and aligned with your ideal clients, attracting the attention of the right people.

If you make a list of all the qualities of your ideal client, or of clients you've worked with that you felt suited your style and capabilities then that's a good start. There's something else you can do too.

Think of all the people you've wasted your time with, people who you thought would buy coaching but didn't, people who said they were interested but weren't, people who took your free sessions and gave nothing in return.

At the end of that sales process, when you knew you had 'lost' that client, you knew that you had known all along that they were never going to buy from you, but you failed to ask the right questions.

As you look back, what were the questions you wish you had asked?

Those are your qualification questions.

12: Opening

Many sales people struggle to close a sale. They might get into a comfortable, technical conversation with the client, or they might be enjoying talking about golf so much that it feels uncomfortable to change the direction of the conversation and ask for the order.

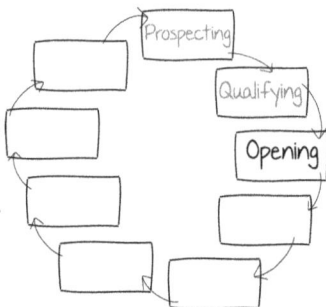

The solution to this is very simple; if you want to close a sales process, you first have to open it.

As a salesperson, you need to drive the conversation from the very beginning.

Opening the sales process means that you are setting the goals and the boundaries for the conversation. You're essentially saying, "I'm talking to you because I can provide a solution to your problem, and at the end of our conversation I expect you to make a decision to buy my solution or not."

12.1   This Isn't a Sales Call...

Some sales people think that clients don't like being sold to, so they respond by pretending that they're not sales people. They're consultants, or advisers, or they're just checking they have the right details for you.

How to Sell Coaching

The problem is that when you start a call by disguising the reason for the call, all you end up doing is confusing and aggravating the client. By being clear and honest, you encourage the client to make an instant decision about whether they're interested in talking to you or not, and either is good.

One of the most effective ways to learn the difference between good and bad sales calls is to actually receive incoming sales calls. If someone makes a bad impression on you, take a moment to think about why. Similarly, if someone does something good, make a note of it.

The problem with sales calls that don't go well is that you have created a poor first impression that is almost impossible to undo. The biggest obstacle to sales calls is that clients don't have a lot of time, so if they don't have time for the first call you make, they're certainly not going to have time for you to explain why you didn't make a good impression the first time.

The earlier you give the client a decision to make, the more you can influence their decisions. Many sales people are afraid of giving the client a decision, because they're afraid that the client will say no. However, the best sales people know that the earlier the client says no the better, because that frees up their time to find a client who will say yes. If your service isn't relevant to the client, there's absolutely nothing to be gained from manipulating them into letting you send them a brochure.

Surprisingly, the most effective opening for an outgoing call is often:

"This is a sales call, do you have two minutes?"

Since time is the single most precious asset of any client or salesperson, the best sales call is one where you get to the point, quickly, and help the prospect to make an instant decision. Acting decisively actually makes it easier for the prospect to say 'yes', because you shorten the time within which the prospect feels uncomfortable because they don't know what you want. By getting the prospect's attention right at the start with clarity and honesty, you gain their 'buy in' to the conversation, which means that they are more likely to want to hear you out.

Remember that the prospect is making a series of decisions which began even before you spoke to them – they decided to answer the phone. They listened to your opening, and then they decided to keep on listening. The decided to either engage with you or put the phone down. They decided that they wanted to hear more. Each decision builds on the previous one, and the more decisions that the prospect makes, the more committed they become to a course of action. Therefore, the best opening is one that gets the prospect to make a decision, such as, "(opening pitch) do you have two minutes to discuss that now and decide if you want to then hear more?"

I'm not saying that this is the perfect opening for you to use, what I'm saying is that you must concentrate on the process of sales, not the magic words. The process will give you the right words.

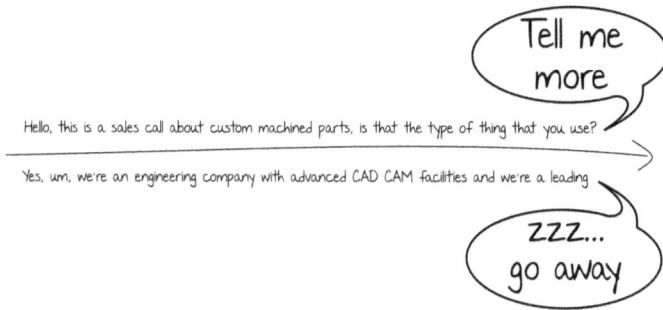

Exactly the same applies to an incoming enquiry call. While the client instigates the call, you must take control of the call right away by asking questions.

Whatever the client's enquiry, there are certain things that you need to know; what they are interested in, delivery requirements, the problem that the client is trying to solve, the impact of that problem and so on.

As soon as you have control of the conversation, you can ask questions which move back through the client's decision process, so even if they start by giving you a technical requirement, you can very quickly move the conversation to a higher level, which increases the perceived value of your solution.

However, the starting point of any incoming conversation is to find out why the prospect is calling.

When the prospect launches into their questions, it can seem difficult, even rude, to say, "Whoa! Hold on there, let me ask the questions first!", so we really need to find a more subtle way to take control of the conversation.

As you'll see shortly, when the phone rings, that might be your first interaction with that prospect but it is not their first interaction with you. Something made them pick up the phone, therefore they have a clear outcome for the conversation – or at least they think they do. They think that they want to either ask some questions or place an order. The problem is that the answers you give them might not be what they were expecting, and they won't be able to move closer to a decision.

Remember that when you answer the phone, the prospect is at a decision point, and they are calling you because they cannot make that decision by themselves. They either need information for their decision, or they need you to act on their decision. Either way, they are calling you because they cannot move forwards to resolve their situation without speaking to you, or someone who they think is like you such as your competitors.

If I call 3 different carpet shops to get a price, I expect to have 3 identical conversations. If you are the only person to ask me a particular question, or offer a suggestion, then you have shifted the balance of the conversation and you will therefore be more valuable to me than someone who just gives me what I ask for.

12.2   What Do You Want?

"Why are you calling?" might sound a little abrupt, and the client probably thinks that the reason they're calling is obvious. However, their reason, as in their expected outcome, is not obvious. They might be calling because:

- They want to get a price
- They want some free advice
- They want to fish for competitive information
- They want to place an order
- They're bored

Once you know why the client is calling, you can find out what it is they need.

Before we begin discovering needs, we should find out more about the decision itself, since we want to keep control of the sales conversation before it becomes a technical conversation, which doesn't lead to an order.

Remember that the reason for every call that you make or receive, and for every meeting that you attend, is to move the prospect one step closer to a decision.

- What do you want to get out of this conversation?
- Are you aiming to place an order today?
- What information do you need to make a decision?

- Have you spoken to anyone else?

- Have you had any other prices?

- Have you bought something like this before?

- Will you need more of these in the future?

- Do you need to open a credit account?

- Can you tell me a little about your business?

- Do you have a website?

The technical discussion then becomes one part of the overall process, one step on the journey.

12.3   Taking Control

12.3.1   Opening questions

Take control of the conversation as early as you can by asking questions. Based on your experience of the enquiries you receive, write down some opening questions that you can use.

Even with a set of wonderful questions to hand, you still might find it difficult to get a word in sideways and get control. The more work the prospect has done before calling you, the more specific they will be in what they ask you for.

If I've measured my living room, chosen the colour, make and product name of a carpet, I'll ring a shop, give them the specification and ask for a price including fitting. Where can they go from there? How can they add value? I've left them no room to negotiate, so they have to try and open up the process again. This seems difficult, countless sales trainers and books make it sound very complicated, and in practice it is so easy that you will fall off your chair when I tell you. Therefore, please sit on the floor now, surrounded by cushions or soft colleagues, to prevent injury and damage to property. Most importantly, put the book on a flat, stable surface so that you don't drop it.

Here's a clue for you. When you answered the phone, you had control of the conversation, and you immediately gave that control to the prospect.

How did you do that?

You invited them to speak.

"Hello, ABC Coaching, how can I help?"

How can I help. How, indeed. Where shall I begin?

The caller will tell you exactly how you can help, because you just asked them to. You gave them control.

Here's a very slightly different alternative greeting, I suggest you try them both and see what happens for yourself.

"Hello, ABC Coaching, my name is Pat, can I take your name please? Thank you Joe, and can I take your phone number in case we get cut off? Great. How can I help you, Joe?"

The pattern of the first example is:

You've dialled the right number, you can have whatever you want.

The pattern of the second example is:

You've dialled the right number, I'll give you some information, then you give me some information, and you get what you want when I invite you to.

The first example is an invitation for the prospect to get what they want – a one way transaction.

The second example is an invitation to trade – a two way transaction.

You take control of the conversation by not giving it away in the first place!

When the prospect calls you, they are not calling you because they have nothing better to do. They are calling you in response to something you have done. You put your phone number in a directory, or on your business card, or on your website, asking people to call you. They are not calling you, they are replying to you. They are accepting your invitation.

I urge you to try out both greetings, and experiment with others too. The pattern I've noticed is this:

Salesperson: Good morning, ABC, how can I help?

Client: I want to order … Can you tell me how much …

Salesperson: Good morning, ABC, my name is … can I take your name? … and your number … and how can I help you, Sam?

Client: I'm looking for … I need some help with …

Can you see the pattern? Simply by making the conversation a two-way trade rather than a one-way reaction, the prospect changes from saying what they *want* to saying what they are *doing*.

This might seem like such an insignificant change, so let me spell it out for you a bit more.

When you open with, "How can I help?" the prospect will take your invitation literally. When the prospect tells you what they want you to do to help them, they expect you to give them only what they ask for.

Since you are then reacting to the prospect, you'll tend to ask for their contact details to "follow up" at the end of the call, if at all.

At the end of the call, the prospect has what they wanted, so why should they give you anything in return? You were happy to give them the information they needed for free, so they want the call to be over as quickly as possible.

When you go shopping, after you pay for your purchases, do you hang around in the shop afterwards? What happens if the retailer puts their 'bargain shelf' after the checkouts, as some DIY chains do? I might often see something I'm interested in, but there's no way I'm getting back into the checkout queue.

The Swedish home furnishings superstore IKEA is an interesting exception to this. What do IKEA place after their checkouts?

Ice creams, soft drinks and hot dogs. Why are these treats *after* the checkouts? Why even have them at all when you've already passed the café upstairs. Because as I said, they are treats, a reward for shopping. You have been a good little girl or buy, here is an ice cream.

When you slow the conversation down and open by trading information, you will hear the prospect respond differently. When the prospect tells you what they are doing, they are telling you about their current situation, opening up space for you to ask questions and make suggestions.

Try it both ways and see what happens.

I'll close this section with one of the easiest and most ridiculously obvious ways to gain control of the conversation. Firstly, remember that you already have control, because you chose to answer the phone, so don't give it away by asking "How can I help?" before you've captured their contact details. So this leads to the question, how do you capture their contact details? You need to record them in some way, yes?

"Let me just grab a notepad... OK, thank you, my name is Sam, can I take your name? ..."

The obvious part? You already had your pen and notepad in front of you.

12.4   Email Enquiries

When you receive an email enquiry, the first thing you have to do is call the client. Assume that they have emailed all of your competitors, and that they can all provide the same service at the same price. The most important factor in winning the business therefore isn't the quality of your response but the **speed**.

Speed is important because the first supplier to respond to the client sets the benchmark by which all other suppliers will be measured.

If you don't already have them, put together some proposal templates for common services so that you can respond with a high quality proposal, quickly.

If you can't send a proposal because you're waiting for information, at least send what you can; a description of your services, case studies etc. Let the enquirer know that you value you them, you appreciate you getting in touch and you are responding.

Whatever you do, remember that the supplier who responds first sets the standard.

12.5   The Most Important Question

There is one question which is even more important than "Why?", and that question is:

> # Why now?

Consider the chain of events:

1.   Client makes enquiry

2.   Client receives information

3.   Client makes decision to buy

4.   Client receives service

Is that what really happens? From your point of view, it might, because that is the window through which you see the interaction.

You receive an enquiry and spring into action, like a finely honed weapon of coaching excellence. However, an enquiry is not the start point of the conversation, the conversation actually started long before this, and the prospect only thought to include you when they were already half way through. Remember that an enquiry is actually a response, because the prospect must have seen, heard or read something in order to know how and why to contact you.

Here's the same chain of events from the prospect's point of view:

1. Something happens

2. Client has a need

3. Client looks for information to fulfil their need

4. **Client makes enquiry**

5. **Client receives information**

6. **Client makes decision to buy**

7. **Client receives service**

8. Client uses service

If we are to generate maximum sales from inbound enquiries, we **must** find out what has made the prospect call now, rather than yesterday or tomorrow. The prospect has taken action because **something has changed**. In sales, we call that the 'compelling event', and we have to find out what that is.

The prospect is not calling to buy your product or service, they are calling to solve their problem, and they are calling **now** because they have their problem **now**. They're not window shopping.

If you aren't relating your service to the prospect's problem, you have no way of making yourself stand out from your competitors.

13: Needs

Establishing the client's needs is much more than getting a list of requirements from them. That tells you what the client is asking for, and I can say that in nearly 30 years, the only times that I've seen clients with purple faces, threatening legal action, is when the salesperson sold them what they asked for instead of what they needed.

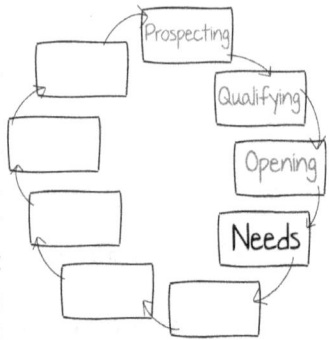

Perhaps the role of marketing is to create problems.

Maybe your teeth aren't white enough, or your washing powder doesn't get your whites white enough, or your house doesn't smell enough like a pine forest.

I didn't know that I had these problems until the TV advert told me so. Marketers have to create problems that their products solve, and in a way, you have to do the same thing.

In product sales, we talk about product features and convert those into benefits, but this is actually a mistake, because the benefit is defined by the customer, not by the seller.

The client's specific problem is revealed by what we have called the 'compelling event', which you know you can uncover with a simple question - "Why now?"

However, this tells you what their problem is, but not their need, which will be more complex, because other people can be involved.

Therefore, you have to convert their need into a tangible value which they can use to convince other influencers who are involved in the decision, and this value also tells you where to price your services.

Working to understand the client's needs doesn't just tell you what they want you to supply to them; it also helps you to understand what they're going to do with it, so that you can:

- Suggest alternatives

- Offer advice

- Warn the client of any potential problems

- Identify new sales opportunities

- Build perceived value in your solution

To discover a client's needs, you have to ask questions. A stereotypical view of sales people is that they are talkative, good at telling people how wonderful their products are. In fact, the best sales people talk much less than you might think; instead, they are good at getting the client talking. And of course, the way that they do that is by asking questions.

> ## Telling is not Selling

By far the most effective way to sell to a client is to ask questions, enabling you to:

- Gather vital information

- Check understanding

- Take control of the conversation

If you don't take control of the conversation then the caller will be in control, they will only ask for the information that they think they need and they will be unlikely to give you anything in return.

As you now know, the sales process is a series of trades. If the caller wants information from you, they have to give you information in return.

13.1   Gathering Needs

As soon as you have control of the conversation, you can ask questions which move back through the client's decision process, so even if they start by giving you a detailed requirement, you can very quickly move the conversation to a 'higher level', which increases the perceived value of your solution.

- What do you need?

- What are you hoping that will do for you?

- Have you looked at other suppliers?

What exactly do we mean by conversing at a 'higher level'? Quite simply, all you're really doing is moving the conversation back to the previous decision point in order to broaden it out and prevent yourself from being rail-roaded into the client's idea of what will solve their problem.

There are many different methodologies for gathering needs, but all you really have to bear in mind is the question, "So what?"

I want a new carpet. So what?

What a prospect wants is not necessarily what they need. As a child you probably wanted ice cream for breakfast, but it's not what you needed. I want a new carpet, but I don't need one. Whatever people say they want is often very different to what they need, and what they go on to buy.

If you ask your prospects to tell you what they want, they will tend to give you a shopping list of the features they'd like, and when you tell them the price they fall off their chairs.

If you ask what they need, you may get a different answer, but it might not be very different.

If we move back to the previous decision point then we're talking about the problem that created the need.

If we move to the decision point before that, we're talking about the compelling event that created the problem which created the need which resulted in the conversation.

You might think that, in coaching, finding the need is easy. The client needs coaching. They need change in their life. They need a breakthrough, a transformation, someone to challenge them to push through their barriers and their self-limiting beliefs, right?

Wrong. These are absolutely not what the client needs, or wants, or will be remotely interested in. These make the coach, in the coach's opinion, sound cool and amazing, but in reality the client wants a problem in their life to go away with the minimum of fuss, effort and pain.

I have found, over the past 20 years or so, that the more the client says they want to transform their lives, the less they actually do want it. Often, they're saying it because they think it makes them sound more committed, and it's often for the benefit of people close to them who are nagging them about their lifestyle or their pathetic failure to live up to their potential.

The client who has experienced a compelling event and has taken this as an opportunity to review their direction in life is the perfect client.

However, if you've built your style and your brand on transformational empowering super charged seismic shift breakthroughs then you're going to actively discourage clients who know that the process of change doesn't happen in one big flash, it happens as a series of small steps.

Small steps seem hard to sell, especially against the noise of the breakthrough empowerment coaches on social media.

However, *everything* is hard to sell when you haven't discovered the client's real need.

The paradox we have, which is explained in more detail in my book Coaching Excellence, is that in the first conversation with a direct prospect, they don't want to tell you their real need because it's personal and potentially embarrassing. The fear which has prevented them from making a change themselves is the same fear that will prevent them from telling you their real need, and is the same fear that will prevent them from getting the results they want with you.

Therefore, the very first thing that you have to do in your conversation with them is reassure them that you are able to help, or not, and that you are on their side no matter what, and that they will make a decision in their own time about what's right for them.

Only when you have soothed their fear might they even consider telling you their real need.

You can find lots of sales courses that will give you the secret questions to uncover needs. A brief search on the internet suggests the following:

> So, what's the one question that will uncover your prospect's REAL needs and wants? It's this: 'How will you know you've made the right choice?'

This is nonsense. It elicits decision criteria, not needs. And this is from someone who says he's a sales expert.

> How would you describe the problem you're trying to solve?
> What about this situation keeps you up at night?
> What challenges have you encountered in the past while trying to solve this?
> How much is this problem costing you personally?
> Is there anything else about the situation that worries you?

They're not too bad, but the client won't give you honest answers because the questions are too direct. They also don't uncover needs, they are actually designed to amplify the problem.

Maybe if you asked them very tactfully, you might get some information. However, as you'll know if you've read Coaching Excellence, the client isn't going to tell you about their problem, they're going to tell you the story that they tell to everyone about their problem. It isn't true, and it justifies them staying where they are, which is of course completely counter productive for the coach.

These questions are all a waste of time.

There's a far simpler question which will get right to the client's needs, and it requires that you do a little detective work first. You know that the client is going to work on a situation in their lives which hasn't emerged overnight. You know that you're not the first person they've talked to. You know that they have been through the loop, many times, of experiencing the problem and either doing nothing about it or self medicating.

Therefore the only question that you need to ask, based on all of this deductive work, is…

"Why now?"

In other words, they could have contacted you at any time, why now? What has happened that makes now the time to finally work on this?

The needs discovery questions above might be more useful when selling to a corporate buyer, however the corporate buyers who you're likely to be selling coaching to will be HR managers, and HR managers are not, by and large, commercial buyers. Unless you're talking to a HR leader in a global corporation, they are unlikely to have complex, multi-level decision making processes, they are unlikely to be writing a business case and they are unlikely to be calculating Return On

Investment. HR managers in small to medium sized businesses are often pushed into working reactively. A manager in the business is likely to have approached the HR manager and said, "I've got a problem with this person in my team, get them some coaching and fix them and if you can't do that, fire them."

When the intermediate buyer is working reactively, they don't have real needs either, because they're not the person with the problem. Now you might see why looking at different sales models was helpful.

What might be the needs of the different people?

End user: None - they're quite happy as they are

Line manager: Get their staff to do what they're supposed to do

HR manager: Get the line manager off their backs and maybe get some hints about becoming a freelance coach

Coach: Make some money

Of course, there are alternatives:

End user: None - they're quite happy as they are

Line manager: Invest in some individual development to support team performance

HR manager: Meet the needs of line managers whilst also reacting to other HR problems

---

Coach: Make some money

You can see that the questions you ask to find out the client's needs are different depending on who you're talking to. The ideal next step in both of the above two examples would be to talk to the line manager because that's the only person who really has a problem, and you might therefore conclude that the line manager is the only person who needs coaching, and I would tend to agree. You might call this an 'upsell'.

We must distinguish between needs and wants. If we break down the real meaning of the words, you will discover something useful and important which will make it far easier to focus on the points which will convert a prospect into a client.

A need is a lack of something which you depend on and which you previously had. Right now, you don't need air, you have plenty of it. But there might come a time when you need air, or water, or sleep, or food. Something which you have become accustomed to, and which is outside of your control.

According to the excellent Online Etymology Dictionary:

Middle English nede, from Old English nied (West Saxon), ned (Mercian) "what is required, wanted, or desired; necessity, compulsion, the constraint of unavoidable circumstances; duty; hardship, emergency, trouble, time of peril or distress; errand, business."

A need is something that you are accustomed to, something that you depend on for survival, and which you may have no direct control over.

A want is a lack, a comparison to what you don't have. How would you know that you don't have something? Because you can see it somewhere, or someone else has it.

Again, from the OED:

c.1200, "deficiency, insufficiency, shortage," from want (v.) and from Old Norse vant, neuter of vanr "wanting, deficient;" related to Old English wanian "to diminish" (see wane). Phrase "for want of" is recorded from c.1400.

What can we conclude from this?

A need tells us that the client is missing something that they used to have.

A want tells us that the client is missing something that someone else has got.

A need tells us what has changed in order to interrupt the availability of something the client depends on.

A want tells us who the client is comparing themselves to, or who is telling them that they are lacking something.

13.1.1 Questions to gather information

List some useful questions for gathering the prospect's wants and needs.

13.2 Recording Information

It's important to have a consistent way of recording the information that you gather because this makes you ask the questions that you might otherwise miss. Are they talking to anyone else? Can they afford your services? What's their compelling event? Oh... I forgot to ask. Never mind.

13.2.1 Recording information

Design an enquiry form to use with every client. If an enquiry comes in by email, the first thing to do is call the client to "confirm a few more details" so you can use this form for either inbound calls or email follow-ups.

13.3 Checking you Understand

Once you've gathered the client's needs, you need to check that you understand them.

When the client is talking through their ideas and requirements, they're rarely doing so in a structured way. When you take control of the conversation, you create that structure.

The simplest way to check understanding is to read back what you've heard to the client.

Let me check that I understand you correctly...

When you check your understanding in this way, the prospect can say one of two things:

- Yes

- No

If they say yes, you've understood them. If they say no, you can explore what you didn't understand. Not rocket science.

In the old days, communication skills training courses used to advocate showing understanding by paraphrasing. This is probably still being taught today, and it's generally a bad idea, because when you change someone's words you're changing the meaning. Your objective is to demonstrate that you understand them, not to get them to understand you. Paraphrasing changes the client's meaning and breaks the rapport that you have developed with them.

"I want a new mobile phone with a big screen and good speakers and a long battery life."

"So you're saying that you would like to upgrade your phone to something with a much better specification?"

"Erm, no, what I said is..."

Some people say that if you only repeat back the client's words, you are only showing that you listened, not that you understood. I say that if you paraphrase, you are describing what you think their words meant to you, which isn't what their words meant to them.

You won't believe me until you've tried it for yourself, so I have devised an exercise which I use during training courses. Here's a transcript of the exercise from a series of training courses for 250 sales people who wanted to be better at getting access to high level decision makers.

Building empathy

Years ago, sales people used to be trained to make small talk with clients. There were sales people who had intimate knowledge of their clients' families, hobbies and golf handicaps, yet they didn't sell anything. We learn by making connections, and those connections often take the form of a purpose. For example, you know what a sandwich is for, so you know how to know when you need one. We do this with relationships, especially those brief relationships that we experience in business. We remember people by what the relationship is for. If the client remembers you as that nice person he talks to about golf, he will come to you for exactly that. If he thinks about your relationship in the context of buying your products and services, that's the track his mind will switch onto when you meet or talk. And if he thinks of you as someone who helps him to solve real business problems... well you can guess the rest. The important thing here is context, so right from the very first meeting, you need to keep your conversation within the context of his business and his business problems – problems that you are going to help him solve.

When people make decisions, their words only rationalise a decision that has already been made, emotionally. By tuning into those emotional signals, you'll know what the client wants they do. If you challenge their opinion head on with facts and figures, all you're doing is embedding the client deeper into their emotional response. In short, your efforts to change their mind actually convince them more.

Let's practice something simple first. In a moment I'm going to ask you to pair up and do a really quick exercise – 5 minutes each is plenty of time for this.

What I want you to do is have your partner tell you about a current, real problem they have that they feel some emotional connection to – maybe frustration, disappointment, confusion, whatever.

You may want to get your notepad and right now, think of a problem you currently have and make a note of it. It can be anything at all – whatever you have in mind write now.

As they tell you about it I want you to ignore their words completely. I know that, as nosey human beings, we like to get tied up in the content, offer suggestions, fix people's problems and so on. Irritating, when people do that to you instead of listening, isn't it! I want you to completely ignore their words and instead focus on only three things, and I want you to notice what they do when they talk about a particular aspect of the problem, or experience a particular emotional state.

What I want you to pay attention to is:

- Their voice tone
- Where they look
- What they do with their hands

That's all there is to it! So, really quickly pair up and I'll call you back in just over 10 minutes. When you're done, stay with your partner for the second part of the exercise.

Feedback from the audience included points such as:

I couldn't pay attention to all 3 aspects, only 1 or 2

Every time my partner said x he did y

I found it hard to not listen to content

He looked around a lot

She moved her hands a lot

His voice tone changed when he talked about his feelings

Now we'll move onto part two.

Go back to the person you worked with last time and summarise their problem back to them to check your understanding.

I want you to each play back your partner's problem, concentrating on using the exact voice tone they used, looking where they looked (as if they were looking at something real) and moving your hands in the same way. If they showed you a direction, or an obstacle, or a picture, just reflect that back. You don't have to understand what it means, you're just respecting the fact that it means something to them. Don't try to understand or summarise the problem at this point. So play back your partner's problem concentrating on their voice tone, eye movement and gestures.

Each take a turn to do that, and again you only need a couple of minutes each.

Feedback from the audience included:

I felt like my partner was really listening

I felt comfortable with my partner

I felt that my partner really understood me

I was surprised that I do all of that when I talk

My partner was very perceptive

What you have done by noticing your partner's voice tone, eye movements and gestures is pick up on the key non verbal communication channels. You have started to focus on the 93% of communication where someone's true beliefs, reactions and intentions are communicated. By focusing on those three things, you will pick up far more valuable information than all of the business plans and organisation charts in the world will tell you.

I think it's a bit unfair that we should spend time exploring your problems and not let you solve them, so the final thing we're going to do is solve a problem only by asking questions about it. Remember, it's not your problem so it's not your responsibility to solve it. All you need to do is change your partner's perspective of the problem.

Think about this in a client scenario. When you are talking to a client who is telling you about a business problem, it matters. It means something to him because he has an emotional response to it. As you're learning during this workshop, the problem isn't really about software compatibility, user capacity or even client satisfaction. The problem is about emotions – triggered by politics, power, threats, perceptions, promotions and so on. If you sit in front of your client and really listen in the way you have practised here today, you will create a greater depth of rapport and empathy than you can imagine. The problem with this is that the client will automatically associate you with the problem – specifically, just because he has told you about it and you have listened, he will think you can solve it.

So let's try out a few questions that we can use to clarify the problem. These questions work in a particular way, changing your partner's perception of the problem. When their perception changes, they will see solutions that had previously been hidden from them. I want you to question the problem using only the questions on the slide. It doesn't matter if you ask the same question more than once, you will get a different answer each time as the problem changes.

If your partner says something that has "I can't" in it, reply with "What would happen if you did?"

You have 5 minutes each for this – and if you solve the problem with the first question, just talk about whatever you like! Remember to ask these questions gently, as if you really care about the person's problem, and as if you know that they already know how to solve it, they just haven't realised it yet.

- What is important to you about solving this?

- Imagine it's a year from now, what feels different?

- What stops you from solving this now?

- What would happen if you did?

- How does a good solution look, sound, feel?

- What do you really want to do about this?

- Think of someone who would handle this really well. What would they do?

- When you look back on this, what seems most interesting to you?

Feedback from the audience included:

It really helped me to think through the problem

It helped me to find my own solution

It changed my perspective of the problem

I feel differently about the problem

Now, you might be thinking that this is all very well for face to face meetings, what about the times when you call someone over the phone? Well, it's exactly the same with just a small difference. This 93% of communication that is unconscious is made up of two components – visual and auditory – which need to reinforce each other for communication to be 'congruent'. We normally perceive congruence as confidence, certainty or honesty. When we speak to someone over the telephone, we only have the auditory component, so where does the visual component come from? We make it up! We make it up based on our own expectations, and on the auditory component.

When you're making sales calls, you unconsciously visualise the person you are calling. If you have never met them, you visualise something based on your prior experience. This is why calls often go exactly the way you intend them to – when you're feeling confident the call goes well, when you are nervous and doubting yourself, the call goes badly.

For the final part of the exercise, I want you to use only your intuition. I know you have a strong intuition, and I know how aware you are of what happens when you trust it, and what happens when you don't. With your partner, I want you to simply trust your intuition. Don't rationalise it, don't explain it, don't find reasons for it. Just tell your partner what you feel their problem is really all about, and give them one single piece of advice. Don't sit there and analyse it. Don't worry about whether it is right or wrong. It doesn't have to make any sense. Just say what you feel is right.

Feedback from the audience included:

The summary was absolutely spot on

My partner discovered something really important that I hadn't even mentioned

The suggestion was really accurate

My partner told me what I already knew I had to do

You see, the 93% and 7% don't just work in the way we communicate outwards – they also apply to the way we take information in. What you have just done, by trusting your intuition, is allowed yourself access to more of your brain than just by focusing analytically. So if you really want to pay attention to someone, stop listening and allow yourself to really hear.

Noticing subtle signals

We've got time for one last exercise, so let's put together everything you have learned so far. I want you to pair up again and imagine that you're making a telephone call to someone who you want to arrange a meeting with. You can do this exercise with your eyes closed if you really want to simulate being on the telephone – that's up to you.

What I want you to do is think of two people now. The first is someone who you find difficult or obstructive, who you struggle to communicate with and who never gives you what you ask for. The second is someone who you get on well with, someone who you feel is always helpful and always sounds pleased to hear from you.

What you're going to do is randomly pick one of those two people and really imagine that you are about to call them to arrange a meeting. Imagine what they look like, imagine their voice and imagine how you feel when you are preparing to talk to them.

As you imagine that person, imagine you are calling them and when they answer, tell your partner whatever you normally say when you make a call. It's not a role play, so your partner does not have to pretend to be that person – you just say whatever you normally say as you imagine talking to the person you have chosen.

Do this a few times, each time selecting one of your two people at random and taking a moment to really imagine talking to them.

Your partner's role is very simple – just listen carefully and guess which person your partner is thinking of. After they have made a few 'calls' tell them what differences you noticed.

Feedback from the audience included:

It was really obvious!

My partner was convinced there was no difference, but I heard it right away

My partner's nervous voice tone made me feel nervous

My partner's confidence made me feel really receptive

We've worked with lots of sales people, helping them to really enjoy making sales calls. One common thing that sales people do is to imagine the person they're calling being impatient or even rude, so they're apologising even before the other person picks up the phone. The solution is to simply imagine you're calling someone you look forward to talking to! The difference in your voice tone will make a huge difference to the state and response of the person you're calling.

So, during this part of the workshop, what have we achieved? Well, instead of hearing just 7% of the client's communication, through their words, we have started to focus on 100% of their communication. It's in that hidden 93% that what they are really trying to tell you is conveyed. By paying attention to that, you will learn more about what is really important to them, and that creates greater empathy and strengthens the connection between you. That strong connection allows you to ask questions that normally you wouldn't get away with, and those questions help you to change the person's perception. Changing the other person's perceptions is the basis for changing their opinions, needs and beliefs, and that is the basis for creating a powerful business relationship.

Through these simple ideas, you can build stronger relationships, influence state and you can change people's minds. You can understand people like never before, and they will want to tell you about what is important to them, because they feel good about telling you. What more could you want!

13.4   What's it Worth?

You've listened to your client with baited breath and now you understand their needs intimately. So what? You know what they need. Big deal. So just sell them that then.

The risk you now face is that it's too easy just to give your client what they're asking for.

A popular sales training model developed by Neil Rackham is SPIN. While observing sales people, he noticed that the best ones asked a lot of questions to help them develop a picture of the client's background situation, their problems and what those problems meant in terms of impact to the business. The final question was to understand what those problems were costing the client's business, so that a 'value proposition' could be made, a proposal with a direct connection between the cost impact of the problem and the cost benefit of the solution.

"So if I could solve the problem of your unreliable photocopier which costs you £100 a year with a brand new photocopier that costs only £100 then after a year you will be saving yourself £100 a year, is that something you would be interested in?"

Obviously, this idea was introduced when £100 was a lot of money. And when there were such things as photocopiers.

The point is that if you don't know what your client's needs mean to them in financial terms, you have no foundation on which to build value. Your carefully extracted needs will just be a shopping list for the client to use to compare you to your competitors.

When you uncover your clients' needs using the method I described above, not only will you understand your client, you will have developed a far deeper connection with them which cannot easily be replicated by your competitors. And if your client is spending time with you, they will be less likely to want to repeat themselves to other suppliers, which gives you a competitive advantage.

14:   Building Value

When you decide to buy something, you compare what the item **costs** and what you feel it is **worth**.

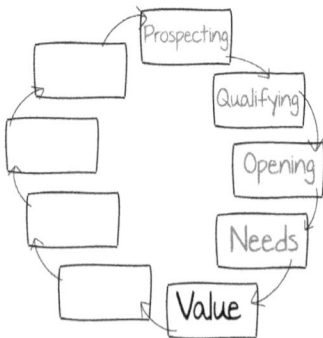

Retailers manipulate this process with discounts and special offers, and 'daily deals' websites manipulate this still further with daily offers of perhaps 70% off the price of something. Unfortunately, they are also playing on your tendency to over-value things that are in limited supply. If you took a few minutes to check other sites, you'd find that you can buy the same thing elsewhere for less than the discounted price.

Clients raise price objections because your price is higher than their expectations, and their expectations are in turn based on their decision process. If you don't influence that process, you have no choice but to negotiate on price.

What are the features of your service that warrant a higher than market price?

- Time

- Relationship

- Quality

- Service

- Availability

- Expertise

- Uniqueness

- Anything else?

Building value in your solution means putting a price on what it's worth to the client to have their problem solved.

This will change the client's response from, "£100?? You must be joking!" to "£100 to solve my problem, that's good value!"

As I mentioned previously, first you have to figure out what the client's unfulfilled needs are currently costing them.

We know that value is subjective, so it will change in comparison to other factors.

Fuel is more expensive on the motorway or at the last service station before the middle of nowhere, and water is more expensive in the desert.

A client will make a decision that they feel most comfortable with when the price that they have to pay becomes equivalent to the value that they will get from the product or service.

When we feel coerced into paying too high a price, perhaps for a house where we thought there was a lot of competition from other buyers, we don't feel good about the decision, and we are unlikely to recommend the supplier to our friends. Similarly, when we feel we've paid too low a price, perhaps for a house where our first offer was readily accepted, we also don't feel good about the decision. We are happiest when we feel fairly treated.

The right time to create a perception of value is therefore as soon as possible, or preferably even sooner.

It's easy to build value when the client is buying a new printer that will save them money on ink. It's harder to build value when the result of buying your service will be intangible. I've seen coaches trying to apply a price value approach, asking their clients to identify the cost of their lifestyle, the cost of smoking, the cost of takeaways, the cost of staying in a job they hate and so on, but this is unreliable because cost is not the incentive for the client to change their behaviour. The smoker doesn't seek hypnotherapy because of the cost of smoking, or at least, not the financial cost.

This also doesn't help when the client's outcome is aspirational rather than remedial. When the client doesn't know how their life could be better, it's difficult to ask them to put a price on it.

Perhaps the easiest approach is to accept that the client already knows what the value of the service is, otherwise they wouldn't be talking to you.

Having said that, you're still concerned about the part where the prospect says, "HOW MUCH??!!"

I've seen coaches charging what are, in my opinion, ludicrous prices for coaching 'packages' which are an attempt to minimise the risk for the coach and increase the order value. In my view, your aim is to reduce the risk for the client, not yourself, and you increase order value by doing a good job so that your clients work with you for longer and refer you to their friends. The way that I've seen coaches sell these packages is to use what you might call 'hard sell' tactics, namely to convince the client that if they delay another moment, they will lose their dreams forever. "You can't afford to wait, you've already wasted too much time, you need to act, you can't let your life slip away" and so on. We are evolved to prefer equality and fairness. We know when a deal is too good to be true. We feel comfortable when we pay neither too much nor too little for something. The client's own goals and desires will move them forwards, you don't need to apply any pressure. What you do need to do is qualify, which means that you have a list of criteria which enable you to identify your ideal client, right at the start of the sales conversation. This helps you to avoid wasting your time and theirs.

I've worked in service sales since the early 1990s and as I may have mentioned already, almost everything that you have read or been told about sales is wrong for selling services like coaching, because almost everyone trying to teach you how to sell is talking about product sales, not service sales.

I first realised this when I worked in the Telecoms industry, for a global service provider. I attended a meeting with some sales people from the professional services part of the business. After listening to the customer describe his business, the professional services people, the 'consultants', said that he should buy a few days of consultancy so that they could do some analysis to tell him how much consultancy he should buy. He declined. They couldn't explain why he needed any amount of consultancy, or what that consultancy would actually give him. He didn't know why he needed it, they didn't know why he needed it.

I came out of the meeting realising that these consultancy experts had absolutely no idea how to sell their service. They couldn't match their service to the customer's needs, they couldn't articulate the value of their consultancy to the customer, and they couldn't even figure out what their proposed solution would look like. I was amazed that these people ever sold anything. To be fair, I think they were used to customers calling them and saying, "Hello, I'd like to buy some consultancy please". But that's not selling, and in practice, it doesn't happen often enough to give you a sustainable income.

Building value is about balancing risk. When the risk of an uncertain future is greater than the risk of staying put, the client will stay put. When the risk of staying put increases due to some external event, which in sales we call a 'compelling event', the client may move forwards, but reactively, and they may not feel good about it. We need to be careful to respect the client's free choice and not take advantage of their moment of need. It will only come back to bite you later.

One way that we can reduce risk is to reduce the size of the steps required to get from wherever we are now to a buying decision. Instead of asking the client to commit an hour to a 'discovery session', ask them for 5 minutes, just to get a feel for each other and decide if they would like a further, more detailed conversation.

By the way, I strongly advise you not to give away free discovery or chemistry or trial or sample sessions. All that you achieve is to let the prospect know that you don't value your time. The idea behind these sessions comes from the mass market life coaching schools, who don't understand the value of coaching. Like the consultants I told you about, they can't explain why anyone would buy coaching so instead they encourage coaches to give a free session in the hope that the prospect likes it and buys more. All that you're really doing is teaching the prospect to expect free stuff from you. Value your time and expertise from the start and you will encourage the prospect to do the same. If they don't, they're not going to be the right client for you anyway.

15:   Solution

We've now reached the stage
in the sales cycle where you
tell the client what you
propose to sell them. You
might do this verbally, or
you might send a written
proposal.

Remember, though…

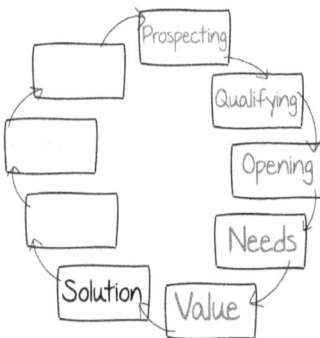

> ## Until the client has a problem,
> ## you don't have a solution

We'll come on to the proposal format shortly, but first
let's look at one of the most typical things you'll hear
sales people talk about; Features and Benefits.

A **feature** is an aspect, quality or characteristic of a
product or service.

A **benefit** is a reason why that feature would be useful
for a client.

A feature of this handbook is that it is *white*. The
benefit to you is that it's *easy to read*.

Almost all sales people are trained to described
features and benefits using the phrase "which means
that…"

"This book is white which means that it's easy to read"

This is the wrong way round, as it creates a break in 'rapport', the sense of harmony and common ground that you have created with your client.

A better way is to use the word "because..."

"This book is easy to read because it's printed on white paper"

Perhaps you're already aware of how your mind runs ahead of what other people are saying to you, filling in the blanks ahead of them. If they are talking slowly, it's easy to get frustrated because you want them to get to the point. This happens because we comprehend language at a number of levels, and each level has a number of possibilities. Your brain is able to make sense of language by trying to predict these possibilities. At the most basic level, the sound of a word might be ambiguous, and until you hear more context, it's difficult to work out the correct meaning.

The words right, write and rite all sound the same but have very different meanings. Even 'right' is ambiguous.

Saying "Feature which means that benefit" makes the ambiguity worse, which leads to discomfort for the client, which can lead them feeling uneasy or uncertain about buying from you.

Here's what happens inside the client's mind:

Feature means benefit:

This book is white...

So what? It looks clean?

which means that it's easy to read

Oh. So it doesn't look clean then.

Benefit because feature:

This book is easy to read

Is it? I need some evidence

because it's white

Oh yes. So it is.

The most important thing to remember about the benefit is that you cannot know the benefit until you have spoken to the client and determined their specific needs. Sales people are usually given generic benefits to talk about; these cannot be benefits to the client because the person who wrote them wasn't talking to the client.

You might be very proud of some aspect of your service, but if the client doesn't care, it's not a benefit to them.

15.1.1 Features and Benefits

Write down the features of something that a client might buy from you, and then write down a benefit for each feature. Then you can switch these around to help create your 'pitch'.

Find a friend or colleague and practice both formats:

- Feature which means that Benefit

- Benefit because Feature

What differences did you and your colleague notice?

15.2 Self diagnosis

As I mentioned earlier, finding out what's in the client's mind is key to your success, and will also help you to get round one of the most common problems that you'll encounter – self diagnosis.

The first thing that most people do when they have a problem is to try and solve it for themselves. Doctors complain of patients searching the internet for their symptoms and jumping to conclusions about their ailments.

What you need to do is get the client to backtrack and tell you about the problem they're trying to solve.

For many service providers, with a prospect on the phone wanting to place an order, this just seems too big a risk. It's easier just to take the client's money and ask questions later.

The problem is that by giving the client what they ask for instead of what they need, you face a great risk that the customer didn't ask for the right solution, and will blame you for selling them the wrong thing.

The customer is not speaking to you in order to buy your product or service, they are asking you to solve their problem, and they are asking now because they have the problem now.

If you aren't relating your product or service to the customer's problem, you have no way of making yourself stand out from all of your competitors.

How do we get round the problem of self diagnosis? You'll recognise this when a prospect tells you what they want to buy instead of telling you about their problem. Remember, people will self diagnose because they are afraid of telling a stranger about their problem. For coaching, a prospect will ask for career coaching instead of sharing how their current employer makes them feel lost, betrayed or worthless and they don't know where they're going in life or if anyone even cares.

Overcoming the challenge of self diagnosis is actually very straightforward. The hard part is doing it with empathy and tact.

Imagine that you work in a hardware store and someone comes in to buy a washer for a kitchen tap. Did they sit there one afternoon and think to themselves, "You know what I'd love to do today? Upgrade the washers in the taps." No.

From the customer's self diagnosis, you can deduce what the problem must have been, and if you have enough experience of the subject area, you can ask questions and suggest alternatives. It's probably the washer, but maybe there are other things for them to check. You might sell some other accessories such as pipe sealant, in which case you have used your knowledge to upsell, or you might give the customer some useful advice, in which case you have used your knowledge to add value to the product.

If a coaching client says that they want to 'take their business to the next level' then you can deduce a few possible preceding steps:

- Their business is at a level

- They are aware that there is another level

- They don't know how to do it

Clearly, something has changed. When they say 'level', are they talking about income, fame, impressing their father, what?

How is this helpful? We know that they have a problem, and that they think the solution is a 'next level business'. We know that the 'level' is meaningless. Who or what is the measure? That's the problem that we need to solve.

15.3   Proposals

Whichever medium you use for a proposal, the format is the same:

Problem

The client's problem or requirement

Cost

What the problem is currently costing the client which might be a financial cost but doesn't have to be

Solution

Your proposed solution

Benefits

The technical and financial benefits of your solution, specific to the client

Value

The price of your solution

Close

Ask for the client's business

You might recognise that this sequence mirrors the decision process that the client has been through.

A written proposal would also include an 'About me' section containing a list of your services and perhaps some examples of clients you have worked with and the problems that you have solved for them. This is where you would put all of those marvellous testimonials that you've been collecting from your clients.

You can even use this sequence to deliver a verbal proposal to summarise a phone call:

"So let me just check that I understand. You have some new staff who don't have sales experience, which is affecting your sales turnover by around £2000 a month, so you're looking for training which will give you the skills you need to close more business quickly. We can provide that for you for £2000, would you like to go ahead with that and set dates?"

"OK, so to check what I've written down, you are finding it difficult to get parts for your old machine, and that's costing you an extra £500 a month in maintenance services, so if we could supply a new machine to you for £2000 then that would give you reliable service and pay for itself in 4 months. Can I send over a contract for you to look at?"

As I said in the table above, the justification for the proposed solution might be financial, but it doesn't have to be. Buyers only need to express a decision in financial terms if they need approval from a finance manager who couldn't care less about coaching or photocopiers or recycling services, they just want to know that the buyer has done their 'due diligence', by looking for answers to some common questions:

- Can they demonstrate that they got good value for money?

- Did they get quotes from other suppliers?

- Was the selection process free from any personal bias?

- Does the solution definitely meet the need or solve the problem?

- What is the warranty or refund policy?

- Have we secured favourable payment terms?

- Did we get a discount?

In other words, the finance manager is trying to minimise the financial risk. They couldn't care less about the coaching service itself. It's not that money is the only thing that matters to them, it's just their job to manage the company's finances.

If you're selling through corporate buyers, you will need to be able to answer these questions. If you're selling directly, perhaps to a private client, you might think that you don't need to worry about such things as money, however that's not the case because ultimately, in every buying decision, money changes hands. That's what makes it a buying decision.

At some point in the process, the prospect has to choose to spend their hard earned cash with you rather than in their favourite restaurant or on a family holiday.

You might try the clichéd, "But you're not paying for coaching, you're making an investment in yourself, in your own future, isn't that worth it?" but you would be forgetting that a lot of people don't like spending money on themselves and are far happier spending it on their families and loved ones. You might therefore try, "But isn't your family's future worth the investment?" and again, nice try, but you're falling into the common trap of trying to justify the price, which of course means that you don't have confidence in the price you've set. If you were fully confident in your pricing, you wouldn't even try to justify it. Your attitude would be 'take it or leave it'.

How does anyone know how much coaching is supposed to cost? The answer is through the process of 'price anchoring', which simply means that the client's expectation is set by the coaching providers. It costs what it costs, and if a client can find it at a cheaper price, that changes their expectations for all coaching. Compare the fees charged by coaches to those of accountants and lawyers and set your fees to be reassuringly high enough to imply quality and confidence.

16:   Handling Objections

A client will raise an objection when you ask for the order and they are not quite ready to make a decision.

If you've read other sales books or been on training courses, you might expect to see objection handling after closing, because that's when the objections typically arise. As a general rule of thumb, if you get objections, then they are either real, in which case you're closing too early and with insufficient information, or they're fake, in which case you're closing too early and with insufficient information.

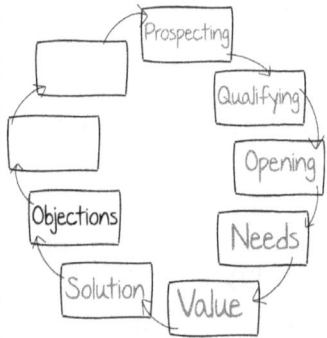

We're talking about objections before the closing stage because you can anticipate and deal with most objections before the client raises them, thereby making it easier to close.

You'll find sales books with objection handling scripts. As I've said previously, scripts don't work when only one of you has the script. It's much better to learn the principles so that you can figure out what to say in each unique moment. Where I've made suggestions, that's all they are.

Your client is likely to raise an objection because:

How to Sell Coaching

- They don't want what you're selling

- The facts of your proposition are unclear

- The needs of the client are not defined clearly enough

- The benefits of your solution are not matched closely enough to the client's needs

- Your client has a concern which, unless resolved, means they will not go ahead

Typically, there are three types of objection:

- True Objections

- Rejections

- Stalls

True Objection

A true objection arises when the client imagines buying from you, therefore a true objection is a *buying signal*.

A **specific question** relating to a specific piece of information that you have just given your client is likely to be a true objection.

A **request for more information** on a particular subject shows engagement and is likely to be a true objection.

A point raised to **dispute the accuracy** or validity of your facts is likely to be a true objection. Your client is seeking factual clarification, rather than blocking you with emotion.

Almost any **specific discussion about money** is likely to be a true objection. Your client is asking you to make it affordable for them and they wouldn't do this unless they were interested. "Can I have a discount?" is not a specific discussion. Saying, "I had £3,000 in mind" is.

However, a price objection means that you have not built sufficient value to support your price, and if you wait until you're ready to close, it's often too late to correct because the client's expectations are already set. If the price objection is non-specific then your client may be using the 'Mother Hubbard' or a similar rejection to see what they can get away with. Don't under-estimate this ruse, I've heard of buyers for a major supermarket using it for an IT services contract worth £14 million. Apparently, as the buyer was about to sign the contract, he said, "Ah, small problem, we don't have £14 million. We have £10 million. Take it or leave it."

Rejection

You may experience a feeling of rejection when:

- There is no logical explanation offered by your client for their negative behaviour

- There is no substance to your client's counter argument

- Your client seems to be working hard at NOT engaging in conversation with you

- Your client seems interested, then reveals they have no budget

- You feel hurt, frustrated or upset

Stall

Towards the end of the sale, when the client is being asked to make a decision, they might use stalling tactics to buy themselves time to think.

A client might stall when:

- They are not motivated enough to buy

- They cannot justify their decision

- They are not the real decision maker

- They think a delay will force a price drop

Negative questions

- How can you justify...?

- What happens if...?

- How does it work when...?

- But...?

- Can't I get that cheaper elsewhere?

- Aren't they unreliable?

The client's tone of voice is negative and they are essentially saying, "I don't agree with you". However, by asking a question, they are giving you a chance to change their mind. The client is saying, "This is what I've heard, is it true?"

While the client may sound negative, remember that they are giving you an opportunity to change their mind. The alternative is that they keep quiet and take their business elsewhere.

Negative statements

We are usually more comfortable with questions than with statements. Questions give us something to answer. Statements make us feel under attack.

When your client makes a threatening statement, turn it into a question that you can answer.

"I don't like the idea of having to change suppliers."

"What is it that concerns you about finding a better supplier?"

When turning round an objection in this way, the one question to avoid at all costs is "Why?"

"Why?" will get the client to reinforce their statement, especially if it isn't a true objection.

Instead of thinking, "Why?", think, "How?" or "What if?"

Once again, by raising the objection, the client tells you that they are engaged in the sales process. The alternative is that they nod politely and then go to your competitors.

16.1 Preventing Objections

- Cover the benefits before the client has an opportunity to raise the objection

- Focus on the positive

- Sell the client what they really need and want as opposed to what we *think* they need and want or what they *ask* for

- Be honest about any potential downsides

- Ask yourself, "Would I buy it?"

How to pre-empt objections

- Before talking to your client, take a guess at the objections they are likely to raise

- Research solutions to the objection

- Work out the positive interpretation

- Raise it as a benefit statement before the objection comes up

For example, before your client says...

"Your company is too small."

You can say... "As we're small we deliver a more personal service that you won't get elsewhere."

16.2   Handling Objections

If you do receive an objection your first response should be neutral support:

- I'm glad you asked me that because…

- I know that's important to you and it's important to me too…

- That's a good point because…

Cost objections can seem difficult to overcome because:

- You know that your competitors could undercut you

- You know what your profit margins are

- You know you just made the price up

- You want the business

- If the client's cupboard is bare, there's nothing you can do about it

But if the client didn't have any money, they wouldn't be enquiring about your services. We all want the best possible product at the lowest possible price and we all love a bargain, but we also know that you get what you pay for.

In your line of work, a poor quality component could be a life-or-death matter, so if you believe in the quality of what you deliver, don't be afraid to ask a fair price for it.

Dealing effectively with the cost objection is as much about your attitude as it is about your skills. Start by accepting that objecting on the grounds of cost is a fairly natural reaction from someone who does not understand the value to them of what you are offering.

> ## ANY cost is too expensive if there is a lack of perceived value

When bottled water was first sold in the UK, in the late 1980s, people laughed. Why would you pay for water when it flows freely from your kitchen tap? The drinks companies have slowly created a perception of value in pure, mountain filtered, organic, healthy water to the point that most people will buy bottled water rather than fill a flask from their kitchen tap.

One global drinks company even made their water sound better because of their pioneering 'reverse osmosis' process, because most people didn't realise that meant the water was filtered from sewage. When people did find out, the company changed its marketing message quite quickly.

Price objections can arise because:

- The client wants to 'win' the argument and prove their negotiation skills

- The client doesn't want to be exploited

- The client knows from experience that bargaining works in getting prices down

- There is an objection that the client has not yet raised, so they use cost as a stall

- The client does not value what you are offering

Handling Price Objections

To find out what's behind a cost objection, ask direct questions such as:

"Are you concerned about the service you will receive?"

Focus your client on goals and objectives. Get them to remind themselves what they are aiming to achieve, and keep their attention on value rather than price.

"What would be your ideal solution?"

"What's most important in your decision?"

Price is rarely the deciding factor in any sale, because for price to be a decision criteria, the client must have a choice of identical products. If you want to buy a new camera then you can shop around for the exact same model and choose the cheapest supplier. But with your service, the client can never make a like-for-like comparison, because features of your service include relationship and expertise which are unique to you.

If you really want to give a discount, position it as a reward for making the right decision, not as an incentive. Always offer a discount with an "If..." statement.

16.2.1 Common objections

Plan for the most common objections that you come across.

Be honest here - what are the objections you've heard, and what objections would you think of if you were buying your service.

Are these objections real? If they are, what can you say to help the client with their decision?

17: Closing

I've put closing at the end of the cycle because that's the point at which the client is ready to place an order and your interaction with them shifts from helping them to make the right decision to actually delivering what they have ordered.

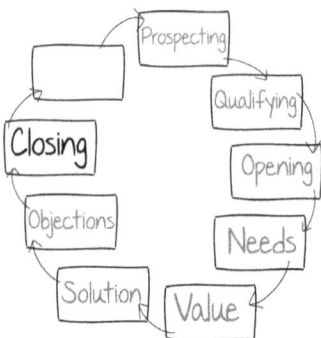

In reality, closing happens at every stage of the sales cycle, because at every stage, some leads are being qualified out and you're focusing more on the ones that you have a better chance of winning.

In order for you to provide a service, you have to do something that your client is either unable or unwilling to do for themselves. Your service can sound great, your references and testimonials can look good, you can clearly understand your client's needs but in order for you to provide your service, you have to start interacting with your client's property. If you're cleaning their windows, you have to put your ladder on their drive and actually do the job. If you're training their sales people, you have to spend time with their sales people. This is the point of greatest risk for the client. What if you break their windows, or drop your ladder on their car? What if you tell their salespeople something that's wrong, or counterproductive?

How to Sell Coaching

Many clients will try to solve this imbalance of risk by standing over your shoulder and watching you. Where you're interacting with their staff, they might even interrupt you and correct you. If this happens, it's a simple sign that the client doesn't completely trust you. Maybe something happened to make them go ahead before they felt totally comfortable, for example they might have been under some time pressure to solve their problem.

What we need to do as we reach the end of the sales cycle is to gain commitment. This could mean that we have to break the project down into smaller chunks that the client feels comfortable with. If you're selling training, you can easily start with a pilot session, which of course you design to ensure that the project goes ahead.

If you're asking the customer to sign the contract, you might include a clause that allows the client to back out if the first stage of service delivery doesn't give them what they need.

This might seem that it puts more risk onto you, but consider that the alternative could be that you deliver all of your service, and then the client doesn't pay you because they're not happy. You would have to take them to court and prove breach of contract, which would depend on the client's perception of your service, and most service providers don't bother, they just write off the debt. If you do go to such extreme measures, you can be sure that you'll never work with that client again, nor anyone who they know.

As with every other stage of the sales cycle, you're balancing risks. When the client's perception of risk matches their expected benefit, they'll move forwards, and the same applies to you too. You also need to feel comfortable working with a client, and that comes back to qualification, and identifying the kinds of clients who you want to work with.

If you're focusing on clients who are right for you, you'll feel more confident, and that confidence will rub off on your clients.

Whilst it's true that both you and your client are balancing risks throughout the process, the client's sense of risk is heightened the closer they get to making a commitment, because a commitment feels like it's a final step that they can't back away from. Therefore, you have to focus on making this step as easy as the first, with low risk and where the client feels in control of the process. That doesn't mean that you tell the client that they can back out any time they like with no hard feelings, it means that you clearly explain what you're going to do at each stage, what the outcome will be and what you expect in return.

Remember, in coaching, the fear that is causing the client's problem will also manifest within the sales conversation and has the potential to derail the process. One of the most important things that you have to do throughout the entire sales cycle is to reassure the client, and one of the easiest ways is not to tell them, "Don't worry, it will all be fine" because for that, they have to believe you. Instead, tell them where

How to Sell Coaching

they are, what's happening and what will happen next. Give them a concrete reality to orient themselves to and they will feel in control and therefore safe.

For example, if you're selling training services, you might tell the client that, with their agreement, you'll start the design process, and the outcome of that will be a training design with some handouts. The next sensible step would be to show those handouts to the client. You might worry that if they don't like them, they'll ask for changes which means more work for you. However, if you don't do that then the client is going into the training delivery with no idea of what to expect, and their sense of risk will be greater, and they will be more critical.

If you show them your design and handouts, the chances are that they won't change anything, but they will feel more comfortable that they are involved in the process. If they do spot anything that needs to change, that's good for you, because the service that you deliver will be more closely matched to what they need.

Imagine that you're selling gardening services. If you agree a scope of work and a price with your client, the conversation doesn't end there. You still need to explain to the client exactly what you're going to do, and make sure that you do exactly what you promise. If you don't, the client will be more likely to be watching over your shoulder or checking up afterwards, and their heightened sense of risk will mean that they will look more critically at your work.

If you explain what you're doing and give your client a chance to have their input, they will feel more confident, and they are more likely to back off and leave you to do your job, and to trust your judgement and expert advice.

The more that your client trusts that you're going to do what you've promised, the more comfortable they will feel, and the more committed they will feel to working with you. Doing what you say you're going to do isn't limited to delivering the main outcome of the service, it applies to every promise you make - when you'll call them, when you'll email them, what you'll send them, what your terms of business will be and so on.

The more your service is tailored to the specific needs of a client, the more you will adopt a consultative approach during the sales cycle.

> **In a consultative sales process, the more talking the client does, the more likely they are to buy.**

If you are balancing the risks at every stage of the conversation, and you are providing reassurance by consistently fulfilling your promises, and you are treating the prospect with tact and empathy, and your services are reasonable priced then there seems to be no reason for the prospect not to say, "Let's do it!"

How to Sell Coaching

and therefore there is no need to specifically 'close the sale'.

However, you will also find that the more control you take of the sales process, the more your prospect is happy for you to lead, and that means that you have to give them the final nudge to sign the contract. You will also occasionally find that some prospects just like to be asked.

You will find books of closing techniques, here are a few that you might come across.

17.1   Common Closing Methods

Direct – simply ask for the business

- Would you like to go ahead?

- Do you have everything you need to go ahead?

Trial – a test for understanding

- How does that look to you?

- How does that sound?

- How do you feel about that?

Alternative – offering a choice

- Do you prefer online or face to face?

- Do you need to set up an account or pay on invoice?

Assumptive – confirming a detail

- When do you want to start work?

- Do you want me to send you ideas for preparation work?

Do you actually need closing 'techniques'?

What we could say is that, since the prospect will place an order at the point that the risks balance out on their decision to part with their cash, the prospect will in fact 'close' the deal themselves. When the prospect is at that point, they know that they want to go ahead and buy, but they don't know how to go ahead and buy, because they are not the expert in your ordering processes – you are. So at that point, the prospect needs to know what to do next. Since we all want to predict the future in order to have a sense of security, you can talk your prospect through the ordering process.

"If you want to go ahead, the next step would be for me to take a few details from you, then I'll call you when the carpet is in stock, which normally takes around 3 days, and I'll arrange a time with you for the fitters to come to you, and they'll take no more than 2 hours to fit the carpet."

"If you're ready to go ahead, I'll get a scope of work document over to you and once you've agreed that, we'll arrange dates to make a start."

At every decision point in the process, what the prospect wants is **reassurance**, and when money is about to change hands, they want that more than ever.

17.2   Reinforcing the Decision

Remember to emphasise:

- They have made a good choice

- The process from here on is simple and hassle free

- You are available for any questions they may have

- You appreciate their business

- They will get real benefits from working with you

17.3   Setting Expectations

As soon as you close the sale, the very first thing you need to do is set the client's expectations by talking them through what will happen next.

Partly, this is about moving them into 'owning mode', and partly it's about reassuring them that they have made the right decision.

Buying a service is inherently risky, because you don't get to find out how good the service is until you've bought it. If things don't work out, you can always ask for a refund, but you've already lost the time that you invested. Many clients stay with poor suppliers in the hope that things will improve rather than go through the pain of finding a new supplier.

While reassurance is important in any decision, in a service sale it is absolutely critical, especially just after the client makes a buying decision, because they want you to prove that you know what you're doing.

You will achieve this by confidently walking the client through the post-sale process.

17.3.1 What's next

Practice completing the following sentence, focusing on the details that will give the prospect reassurance that you know what you're doing, you have done this before and they are in safe hands.

"Thank you for choosing to work with me. What's going to happen now is..."

17.4 Contracts

Should you get your client to sign a contract?

There are perhaps two schools of thought.

One says that a written agreement is needed in any transaction to make sure both parties are clear about their obligations.

Another says that in most countries, a verbal agreement has the same validity as a written contract. If you're in a country where that's not the case, they're probably not going to care about a written contract anyway. In any case, if you ever have cause to look at the contract, the relationship is already in trouble.

A contract will contain two main parts. The first is your general trading conditions, such as payment terms, confidentiality, termination, ownership of intellectual property, dispute resolution and so on. The second is the scope of work which defines what you are delivering to the client and what they are paying you for it.

Personally, I think that a written contract of some form is useful, even if it's just a summary in an email, because it sets out in recorded, dated text what the client is letting themselves in for. It's a final check that they really are ready to go.

I'm not going to give you a contract template as there are many free and paid resources online.

A scope of work would include things like:

- The number of coaching sessions
- The typical duration of a session
- The location or format of a session
- The cost
- The payment terms
- Any deliverables or metrics

Overall, the scope of work answers the question, "What am I getting for my money?"

Your terms and conditions allow you to set out your expectations, so this is where you would include your cancellation policy and any restrictions, such as the disclosure of mental health conditions.

If you are raising invoices for your client to pay against, you would then refer to the scope of work on your invoice, especially if you're splitting the overall project into a number of stages. On your invoice, you would also include a Purchase Order number or supplier reference, if they've given you that. These details make it far easier for a corporate client to pay you without delay.

I find that private clients rarely ask for invoices, but they do ask for receipts when they realise that they can claim the costs against their tax bill.

18: Follow Up

One of the most difficult
things to get sales people to
do is follow up. Many are so
grateful to get the client's
order that they daren't go
back and ask for feedback in
case the client changes their
mind!

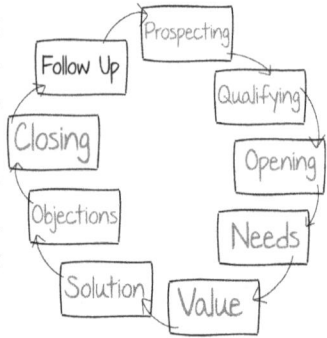

For large orders, it's more common for sales people to
ask why they lost.

Hardly any sales people, only the very best ones, will
call a client to ask why they won an order.

Following up serves a number of purposes:

- Learn what you did that worked so that you can
  do it more often

- Learn what you can improve on

- Reinforce the client's decision

- Build a long term relationship

- Get testimonials at the point where the client
  feels good about their decision

Questions to ask include:

- Why did you choose to work with me?

- Why did you choose to give me your business?

- How would you like me to keep in touch with you?

- Are you happy with the service you received from me?

- What could I have done better?

- Would you be happy to be a reference client for me?

- What advice would you give anyone who is thinking of working with me?

- Would you be happy to write a brief testimonial to help other clients make a decision that they are happy with?

18.1 Testimonials

When is the best time to ask your clients for testimonials?

Surely, after you have delivered an amazing coaching program and transformed their life?

No.

This might seem counter intuitive at first, so stay with me. The best time to ask your client for a testimonial is after they have committed to work with you and before you have actually had a coaching session with them.

Crazy, eh? Hear me out.

At what point does a prospect care about your testimonials? At the decision point. Not before and not after.

At that decision point, what does the prospect need reassurance for? Their buying decision.

At the decision point, why would the prospect care about how you've transformed someone else's life or how you've helped someone else have a breakthrough? This isn't where the client is in the process. What they want reassurance about is "Am I making the right decision?"

A client of mine who is also a coach had an interesting experience. A prospect contacted her via social media and after a conversation, decided to go ahead with coaching. The client then started posting on social media sites about what a great coach my client is. Why? In order to justify her buying decision and minimise her perception of risk. When you make a decision that you don't feel completely sure about, what do you do? You tell your friends and colleagues to see if any of them say, "YOU DID WHAT????"

At the moment of decision, the prospect wants to be reassured that they are safe. Just beyond that point, the client feels their maximum level of certainty, and that's the time for them to share their story.

The testimonial isn't, "Peter is an amazing coach and changed my life", it's, "Here's why I chose Peter as my coach", because that's what the prospect most needs to know about.

All of your testimonials will otherwise be glowing endorsements of your skills as a coach. The prospect already knows that, otherwise they wouldn't be talking to you. They also know that you're unlikely to share bad reviews. What they need reassurance about is their decision to move from your prospect into your client.

18.1.1 Create a schedule

For each client, you can create a follow-up schedule to make sure you stay in touch and pick up any future opportunities. You could also set up automatic reminders in your calendar software.

- 1 hour
- 1 day
- 1 week
- 1 month
- 3 months
- 6 months
- 1 year

19: Account Management

When you begin to routinely follow up and keep in touch with your prospects throughout their decision cycle, you have become an Account Manager.

Account management is the set of activities required to build a long term commercial relationship with a client.

Some sales people thinking that visiting a client on a regular basis for a 'catch up' is account management. Other than the fact that you're talking to an existing client, your approach should be exactly the same as for dealing with a new business lead; you have to qualify the lead, drive the sales process and help the client to make the right decision.

You already know the client's general requirements, but don't allow that familiarity to make you complacent and assume the client will automatically place an order with you.

Probably the most important feature of account management is that an existing relationship gives you a reason to contact a client and find out about their future plans. This enables you to influence their decisions and discover opportunities for services that you can provide, but which the client doesn't know you can provide. This is called 'cross selling'.

When you anticipate a client's needs before they talk to potential suppliers, you can solve the client's business problems rather than just responding to their technical requirements. This automatically makes your service more valuable to the client and locks out your competitors. This approach is often called 'solution sales'.

Think back to Jim Holden's 4 level model. Where does an account manager fit within that? Level 4? Not usually. Level 1 is usually not sufficiently focused on the sales target. Levels 2 and 3 are where you'll find most Account Managers, because these are the levels with the target and relationship focus to develop an account relationship.

I'm not going to say a great deal about Account Management because it is quite straightforward, in principle at least. Rather than looking for new prospects through 'cold' lead generation, the Account Manager focuses on prospecting with existing clients. Fundamentally, the Account Manager has to add value to the client and he or she achieves this by having something to say to the client other than, "Have you got any orders to place this month?". That's Level 1 order taking, it is not Account Management.

There are broadly two types of Account Manager.

19.1 Service Account Management

A client who buys a service from you, such as equipment maintenance, internet access or property management, will have an ongoing need for information about the performance of their service. The Account Manager uses these service conversations to find out about new opportunities and also competitive threats.

The biggest threat to this type of account is the supplier's own complacency, which can create an opening for a competitor to offer better service levels or more attentive Account Management.

If you're running a large coaching program, or if you have a team of associates working on a large program, your regular meetings with the buyer or main stakeholder will give you an opportunity to create value, build the relationship and find out about new opportunities.

19.2   Commodity Account Management

A client who regularly buys commodities from you such as cleaning products, electrical components or raw materials will have to place regular orders. Rather than simply filling in the order form, the Account Manager uses these conversations to up-sell and cross-sell and also find out about competitive threats.

The biggest threat to this type of account is price, and the Account Manager can counteract this threat by providing added value to the client, perhaps in the form of education, access to product development teams or joint marketing. The Account Manager might also help the client with 'emergency' orders, something which the client might not get from a cheaper supplier where they are just another client.

19.3   Account Development Plans

Perhaps the most important tool for an account manager is an Account Development Plan, which is simply a way of documenting what you know about a client and what you plan to do with that knowledge to achieve your commercial goals.

What information should be collected in an ADP?

Current Knowledge:

- Business description

- Contacts

- Market analysis

- Client's competitors

- Account activity to date

Account Potential:

- Future plans

- Organic growth

- Cross selling

- Referrals

- Revenue potential

Account Plan:

- Short and long term strategy to realise account potential

Create your own account plan template that contains the information you need. It's a good idea to keep this at the front of your coaching notes and keep adding to it as you learn more about your client. You can see that this is incredibly valuable when you're working with corporate clients, and it reminds you that even once you've 'won', the sales cycle never ends.

19.4 Client Care

Imagine that you've done your job, you've delivered your service, now what? Are you onto the next client? Back to marketing?

You'll remember that the best sales people know that their existing clients are the cheapest and best source of new sales leads, either for repeat business or for recommendations.

This is a dangerous time for you as a service provider, because you will feel compelled to give your client more than they have asked for in order to create the sense that you have delivered great customer service.

Remember the research from the University of Maryland into the value of customer service.

What they found was that the more companies spent on customer service, the greater their customers' perception of service. No surprises there.

So, companies that spent money on nice waiting rooms for customers, or who offered free extras, or maybe hotels that gave their guests nice toiletries and chocolates benefited because their customers thought that the service was better than that of their competitors, and so their customers were more loyal and spent more, and profits went up.

However, there came a point when spending more money reversed the effect on customer service. When companies spent more and more money on things that affected service, their profits actually went down.

What the researchers found was that when customer expectations were met, or very slightly exceeded in the areas that were important to them, they perceived a high quality of service. But when the service provider did something that made no difference to the customer, the cost of providing the extra service reduced overall profits with no benefit.

This is something I've noticed many times with a wide range of service providers. For example, if I take my car to be serviced at a main dealer, they might give me free drinks and snacks, but as a customer I don't want to be in the garage long enough to enjoy them! I want to drop my car off and pick it up in the absolute minimum of time. So they would be better off spending that money on something that will save me time, which is more important to me.

On the subject of time, the garage might call me and tell me that my car is ready an hour ahead of schedule, thinking that I'll be pleased. Actually, I feel the opposite because I've planned my day around the time they gave me. I'd rather that my car is ready when it's supposed to be ready.

Another example is where a service provider gives me a discount because I had to wait. If I didn't mind waiting then all they've done is give away profit. It doesn't make any sense. Of course, I'm happy to take the discount, but I didn't need it and I didn't ask for it.

Therefore, the golden rule is to not assume what your clients perceive as examples of good service.

When we have companies like Amazon and eBay offering free delivery, no questions money back, next day or even same day delivery, it doesn't only affect other online retailers, it affects everyone. When retailers try to steal market share with these kinds of features, they change the customer's perception of what to expect from every service provider. Now you'll see instances of free delivery reducing, as retailers realise they can't carry on absorbing those costs.

Don't be tempted to give your clients more than they have asked for in the interested of providing 'good service' - remember that if the client doesn't have a problem, you don't have a solution. Stick to what the client is fundamentally expecting from you. If you're cleaning their oven, make sure their oven is clean. If you're mowing their lawn, make sure their lawn looks good. Take away all the cuttings, rubbish and so on. Put all your tools away and only then ask the client to take a look. If you're coaching, keep checking that your conversations are meeting their needs and that they feel that they are moving in the right direction.

How to Sell Coaching

Think about presentation. You don't need to show them how hard you're working or how busy you are. Who cares about that? They want to see that you have done the job that they expected and paid you for, and they came to expect that service because that's what you told them you could and would deliver. So only set expectations that you are confident in living up to.

Caring for your client means, simply, doing what you said you would do.

Beyond that, you might think about other things that they might find interesting or useful. You might email them an article that you found, you might send them some survey reports. You might send them some kind of voucher about an additional service. In other words, you find ways to keep in touch with them with information that they might find useful.

If you want them to give you referrals, make it easy for them. Give them business cards to give to their friends, look out for referrals that might be of interest for them. Let them know about upcoming events or conferences that they might like to attend. Keep it relevant to them, and you start to create the perception that you can add value, that you are more important than the service you provide.

Finally, the simple golden rule of good service is this: Treat your clients as you would want to be treated.

20: How to Get More Clients

So, how *do* you get more clients?

You sell more.

Let's break that down into something a little more specific.

1. Find out where your target clients are and make sure they know you exist

2. Respond quickly to enquiries

3. Get out there and meet people

4. Qualify your prospects, protect your time

5. Measure your progress through the sales cycle

6. Find ways to improve your conversion ratio at each stage of the sales cycle

7. Stop spending time on activities which don't increase conversions

8. Track cashflow, not money in the bank

9. Look after your clients as buyers, not just consumers

10. Repeat

I think that's about it. I've been personally involved in the professional sales arena since 1988 when I first started giving customer demonstrations and presentations and working closely with sales people. From there, I moved into an area called 'pre-sales' which you could say is the technical part of the sales role, and from there into 'solution sales' which means selling big complicated things, and from there into starting my own business in 2002, or really 2000 if you count the time that I was building my own business whilst still being employed in the telecoms industry.

I've worked with hundreds of sales people over those years. Some were terrible and never moved past level 1. Most, by definition, were average. They did OK when the economy was good. They survived by being in the right place at the right time. Some were exceptional. To watch them at work was like watching a genius, a maestro, a master, a wizard, a ninja. And thanks to my skills in modelling intuitive talents, I captured the essence of their abilities and condensed them into this book for you. To them, I am indebted.

Sadly, though, I can't do your job for you. The best person, by far, to sell your services is you.

Get on with it.

21: About Peter Freeth

Peter Freeth has worked with corporate and SME clients since 2000 to deliver the highest levels of measurable business performance through people development:

- 700% increase in profitability through coaching Parker Hannifin's leadership team

- Enabled the sales director of Logica to deliver £300,000,000 in new business revenue

- £16 Million in lost revenue identified and recovered for Babcock, arising from project mismanagement and poor management controls

- Doubled sales conversion rates for Domestic & General through trainer training

- Doubled sales conversion rates for Fitness Industry Education through sales coaching

- 25% time and cost saving on Somerfield's graduate training program, achieved by identifying and 'blueprinting' the talents of high performers within the business

- 83% success rate for career promotions for 25 'future leaders' through a succession planning program at Babcock

- Coached the sales team of FGI Mercer from 50% of target to all being over target

- Trained 250 of BT's SME sales people in how to get access to a decision maker

- Trained 200 of RSSB's staff in how to engage and influence stakeholders

Peter has written 14 books on various business and leadership subjects as well as countless magazine articles. He has presented at intentional conferences in Poland, Ukraine, Denmark, USA, Canada, South Africa, Turkey, Europe, North Africa, Ireland and the UK and is an expert in creating high performing cultures through leadership excellence.

Peter's books are all based on insight and experiences gained from solving real business problems for clients.

Join Peter's mailing list at nenlp.com

Learn more about Peter's work at genius.coach

Change Magic
Peter Freeth

Learning Changes

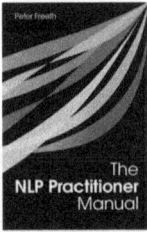

Peter Freeth

The
NLP Practitioner
Manual

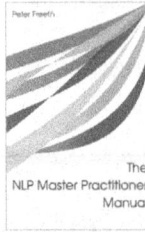

Peter Freeth

The
NLP Master Practitioner
Manual

Peter Freeth

The
NLP Trainer Training
Manual

Coaching
Excellence

Projective
Coaching
Techniques
Peter Freeth

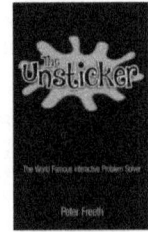

The
Unsticker

The World Famous Interactive Problem Solver

Peter Freeth

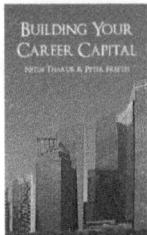

BUILDING YOUR
CAREER CAPITAL
Neena Thacker & Peter Freeth

NLP in Business
Peter Freeth

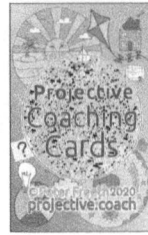

Projective
Coaching
Cards
Peter Freeth 2020
projective.coach